Zen
One Flavor

Aaron Fisher
-無為海-

ISBN-13: 978-1479124138
ISBN-10: 1479124133

For inquiries, contact:

www.the-leaf.org
www.globalteahut.org
www.sagacitea.com

For my beloved wife, my Autumn Fu Ping.

In true Zen form, she sacrificed her time and energy to this work, creating the emptiness within which this book was able to find its form.

Le Thé du Jour

A thousand, thousand cups—
Each one the Morning Dew.

Introduction

Zen is no ordinary religion. It has no prevalent dogma, rites or rituals; there isn't even any coherent soteriology—Zen is an experience! And throughout the ages, masters have used a wide variety of techniques to help instigate that certain sensation in students: a recognition of the fact that the so-called "self" is an illusory construct of social programming and the nature of rational, as well as linear, linguistic thinking. This experience cannot, however, be easily described or conveyed in words, concepts or ideas; it must be lived through. As a result, many of the methods used to catalyze this awakening were also non-verbal; and all-too-often even when they were taught in words, the teachers of old used illogical nonsense meant to show the practitioner the absurdity of trying to achieve a linguistic Zen. More often, the transmission happened quietly and subtly, and wasn't recorded in books or treatises, occurring instead within the realm of personal experience—the space between master and students. And in imagining these ancient gardens, monasteries and forests where intuition was passed on from master to pupil, we invariably find steaming bowls of tea nearby; for since ancient times, Eastern mystics have utilized tea to transmit understanding. After all, what could be more substantial and experiential, as well as symbolic and philosophically profound, than the master brewing his mind into a cup that is passed steaming to the student, who then consumes and absorbs it, physically and spiritually, literally and metaphorically?

They say that the flavor of Zen and the flavor of tea are the same, and without an understanding of one, there is no mastery of the other. The affinity between tea and Buddhism, especially *Chan* (Zen), is a friendship dating back more than a thousand years. In the beginning, tea was always an aspect of spiritual well-being and healing, used first by aboriginal shamans and then later by Taoist mendicants. Learning from these Taoist sages, the early Buddhist monks would also come to adopt the Way of Tea as an important aspect of their tradition. They would then be the first ones to domesticate tea, and also develop much of the aesthetics, pottery and brewing methods that would mature into the artistic appreciation of tea by royalty and literati. All of the famous tea mountains in China also have Buddhist monasteries on them, and this is no coincidence: sometimes the monks or nuns were drawn by the wizened tea trees that grew wild there, while at other times they brought the tea with them.

When tea eventually was taken to Japan by monks who had traveled to the Mainland to study Zen from the masters there, it would also develop into a symbolic expression of the Zen mind in the tea ceremony, called "Chanoyu". These monks came back with Buddhist teachings, tea wisdom, teaware and even seeds and saplings as a testament to the fact that tea was such an essential aspect of practicing Zen at that time that they couldn't establish Zen in Japan without it. But what was this "Zen" that needed tea to take root?

There was to be a sermon on Vulture Peak, but the Buddha only raised a single blossom and held it poised in his fingers. And thus, as Mahakashyapa understood, Zen was established. There is a metaphysical distinction between the "Buddhist" tradition and this mind-to-mind transmission of wisdom, which came to be known as "Chan" in China and "Zen" in Japan, after the Southern-Chinese pronunciation. Despite this division, the ineffable, living Zen is not necessarily mutually exclusive with the tradition of Buddhist ideals and philosophy that shares its name. Many masters have found their wisdom wearing monastic robes, and chosen to keep them on afterwards as a way of exemplifying ideals and sharing their understanding with others. But unlike most spiritual traditions, Zen masters have always been extremely aware of the limitations within their own, or any other, tradition—as if to say: "Zen isn't in the robes, bowls, rituals or even sacred scriptures. Don't look for it here. And yet, if you look carefully, all this somehow points to it."

The life of Zen was unique because it was more about the tea than the usual "sacred" stuff going on at other monasteries. And by "tea" I mean farming and processing, working and sweating, as well as the more poignant preparation of the steaming bowl that was passed around Tang Dynasty monasteries every evening. The real pith of Zen was only real when it was in your marrow, and it only circulated that bone-deeply after years of muscle memory—thousands of buckets of water and chopped wood. And isn't the Way of Tea the same? There's no reading about how to make a cup of tea that shines with the deepest wisdom and most ordinary thirst-quenching satisfaction both. There is no way to say—not with all the ten-thousand words—what precisely it is that tea conveys beyond its flavor and physiological relationship with the body. It takes years of coal and water—kettle after kettle—until the ceremony sinks in and merges with life itself. And yet, it is right here in this beginner's kettle, too. It was there all along.

When the ancients said Tea and Zen were the same flavor, they didn't mean tea as a kind of Buddhist ritual. They were talking about that wordless hush before the Buddha raised the lotus on Vulture Peak. They were talking about Bodhidharma's marrow—given to Hui Ke for the perspicacity of his silent bow—and Hui Neng's sieve. They were saying that all-too-often the essence of Zen is more easily communicated through art and life than it is in words, though it can indeed be instigated by language. You could say that Zen has always been based on the intention of the Buddha and all the masters that followed to cast the light of that one primal illumination: our true self is not this egoic I-subject, and there is no-thing apart from Mind. All the meditation techniques, the moral precepts, the slaps and whacks, the nonsensical gibberish and all the pots and pots of tea have all steeped in this truth, since before anyone ever said the word "Chan".

And so, if tea is Zen and Zen is tea, then this can't be a book about "Zen Buddhism". It isn't a history of the relationship between tea and that tradition. If you're looking to study Zen or Tea, this really isn't your cup of tea. There's nothing wrong with taking an interest in the history of the Zen tradition, or tea lore for that matter, but if you get too caught up in collecting information you can flounder. I only use the name "Zen", actually, because that is the more popular word in English. Despite some propaganda often promulgated in Western Zen circles, "Chan" is very much alive in Taiwan, Hong Kong and China and never really died out, as some would have you believe. But that is just the kind of anecdotal factoid that can trip you up, isn't it?

The "Zen" that is in tea has nothing to do with learning about the dates different teas were grown on which mountain and by which lineage of monks, however intriguing that information might be to the intellect. Neither is it a memorization of old scriptures or biographical sketches of masters. The Zen of tea is a direct, existential change that is changeless, as it leaves no trace. Try to catch Zen and—like a boy playing with the wind—you'll find yourself staring down in wonder at an empty palm. And this Zen has been around forever, eons before the Buddha held up that flower, just like tea has been here since long before anyone plucked and steeped its leaves. There were giant tea trees looming over antediluvian forests with graceful buddha-eyes long before the first human voice shattered the til-then incomprehensible *sutras* being chanted by wind-rustled leaves and yellow warblers.

I'd like this book to pay homage to that living Zen, and just like the pure white porcelain cup, steaming after a rinse, let us also wash off all the Zen Dust we've accumulated—at least while we're here—and just read without arguing this or that tradition or philosophy. There's no arguing with that flower on Vulture Peak, just like there's no arguing with the tea cup—full or empty.

Each of the chapters in this book is a cup of wisdom in and of itself, and could be drunk at any time, in any order. There can be no organization to a discussion about the state of being called "Zen". It's bad enough we have to follow these letters from left to right in linear time—unless you can pause, take a breath and notice the gaps between each word as well, letting the space of the page sink in as much as the words do... I know we'd all like a neat and tidy parcel with an instruction manual inside: "Enlightenment from A to Z-en". But the *real* world is wiggly—and the Truth doesn't respond to ordered, logical, step-by-step analysis. If the secrets to enlightened living could be pocketed, we'd all have long ago transcended this realm. As soon as you think you have found the ideal place to settle, the true Zen master goads you onwards and tells you what you think you've attained doesn't matter—just as the best Zen art leads you ever onwards, deeper and deeper into contradiction at every turn.

Zen art—just like tea art—is always incomplete (*wabi*), incorporating boundless space. Most Zen books are *about* Zen art. But words themselves can also *be* Zen art in and of themselves—and prose as much as poetry or calligraphy. It is my ambition that this book you are holding be *itself* an expression of Zen art, rather than just a topical study of the arts that have been used to communicate Zen throughout time. Consequently, as you read through this collage of Zen-words, homilies, parables and proverbial insights you will see that this book-as-artwork is all tattered around the edges, like any good tea cloth (*cha bu*); and each strand leads unfinished towards other books and teachings—deeper and deeper into Zen. If you're inspired to never read again and seek out a good kettle for tea, I'll have succeeded in my perhaps over-ambitious aims. And yet, I'll also happily settle for a feeling of curiosity that leads on down any number of the unfinished stories, lessons or parables in this book towards other books and teachers greater than I. The mind-pastels in this book are of themselves just divided-mind rambling on and on about whole-mind; but if you step back and look at all the splotches of color from a distance, you may just *identify* whole-mind. Don't get frustrated with the terminology and poetry, deep philosophy or absurd nonsense. Rather, see the grace in the warped bowl and simple, unadorned bamboo tea scoop, letting it all inspire you to brew one more time.

You can turn to any chapter in this book as you can sip from any side of a tea bowl. Just as the experience of Zen is and isn't in the tea, it is and isn't in the words. For the most part we speak what cannot be practiced, and practice what cannot be spoken. I'd therefore recommend a few kettles of tea to go with each of these literary, metaphorical cups. But that's not necessary. The words can point out the Way as the tea can, though maybe not as well. Take a sip from here, or one from there—or perhaps sip all the cups in order. It doesn't matter.

I have gathered together here some of the finest leaves the Zen mountains have to offer: stories, *koans* and even a bit of fiction from China and Japan. Most of them really happened, or are at least scripturally documented; a few were composed out of my own life of tea. I have taken some license with all of them, as the Zen we're looking for isn't about being a stickler to details any more than it is in collecting information. All the dialogues in the annals of Zen history revolve around the same dilemma: show your Zen without speaking and without being silent. Quick!

The answer isn't as important as its source. Each of these twenty-one cups is an answer to that question. The first part of each is the essence of that tea as it is drunk, and then I've added my own commentary for "while the next one is steeping." You are welcome to your own insights as well, and they may be deeper, even more poignant and transformative than mine. Zen stories are often bottomless in that way. But try to set the argumentative mode of being aside: there's nothing to agree or disagree with, merely signs pointing the way. If you don't like a certain kind of tea, toss it out—the dregs will fertilize the plants. There's a whole world of teas abounding throughout this twenty-one cup session, and you're sure to find one that coats the throat and lingers on the breath in that special, quieting way.

If I could, I'd share a cup with every single one of you and we'd together lose guest and host. Otherwise, there's this book, and our shared experience of it—me in the writing and you in the reading. Whatever truths you find floating near the bottom of your cup are yours—they always were.

May you find the tea in your Zen;
And the Zen in your tea.

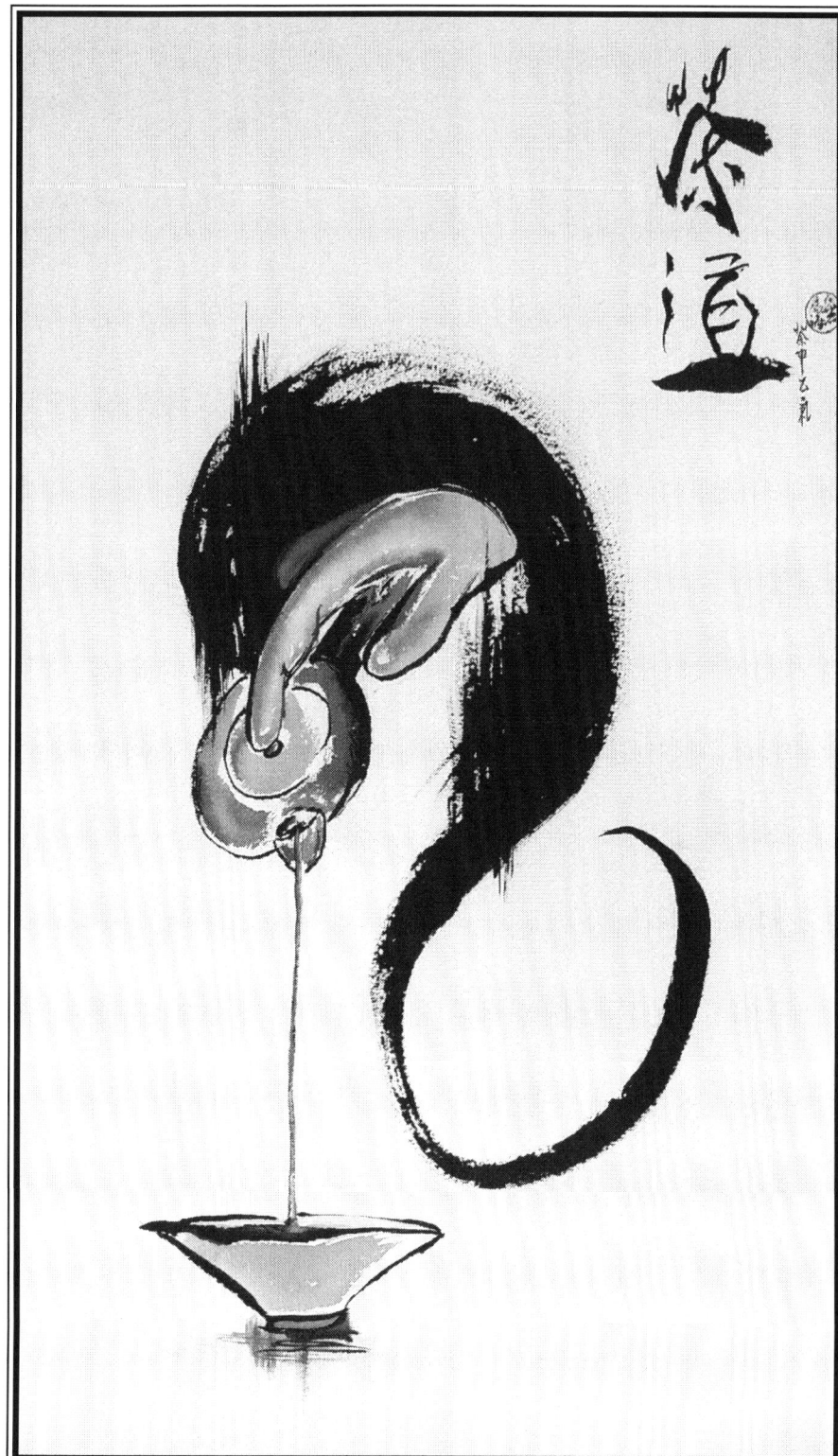

The First Cup
Empty It Onto the Ground

Have a cup

One of the wisest professors at the University of Punditry had reached the end of a long and prosperous career, with an alphabet of letters after his name and a paragraph of awards to put in the small biographies printed on the backs of his many books. He smiled and accepted compliments, pretending to be modest while his face betrayed the fact that he was basking in it all. Despite his intellectualism and the fact that he had lived so disembodied that most ordinary people couldn't understand what he was saying—despite his "elephantiasis of the ratiocination organ" (as he himself would call it), he did deep down wish to understand the Truth, the world and even perhaps himself. He wasn't really content.

He had spent twenty years seeking answers in the library, discussing and re-discussing his ideals over and again in the jargon he and others had created. They sent memos—and later in their careers, emails—arguing the nuances of what "Truth" itself meant (because, of course, one had to establish all that before any real understanding could begin). Now, however, at the end of this long, winding path through academia, he still felt hollow, as if he was in fact no closer to understanding why he was here or what life was about.

A friend of the family was over for dinner one night and described a recent trip to the mountains. He mentioned meeting a monk who lived way up a winding trail in a small temple. He said the monk had become quite famous in the region for his wisdom and perspicacity. The scholar's ears perked up. Perhaps one such as this would have the answers to life. What did it all mean? Is there a God? What happens when we die?...

As he planned for the trip, the scholar made lists of questions—crossing some out with red ink and rewriting them. He then paced his study memorizing them, as it would be unseemly to bring the actual list before the monk. He insisted that his family stay behind in the small village, hiking up the trail himself. After a long, grueling trek, he found the small temple and adjoining cottage.

The monk invited him in. When he said that he had come from far away to ask the monk some questions of the utmost importance, the old man asked him to sit down and insisted that they first drink some tea. This made the impatient scholar a bit peeved, as he had waited so many years and was anxious to test the wisdom of one who hadn't read nearly enough books, but he agreed out of politeness. As the water boiled the old monk glanced out the window at the mountains, and the scholar thought he was being ignored. He used the time to organize his questions in his mind, silently counting them off on his fingers.

When the tea was ready, the monk placed a bowl before the scholar and leaned over with the teapot. His wizened hands were perfectly steady, and the stream of tea poured so smoothly it appeared soft in the dim light—it poured, and poured and poured. Soon the tea reached the rim of the cup. Then beyond. It spilled over the table and splashed onto the mat next to the scholar with a resounding "Hey! What are you doing?!" The old monk set the pot down gently and gestured to the brimming cup with his eyes, "Your mind is like that cup, so pray tell me: Where am I to pour the wisdom you seek?"

While the next pot is steeping

Is your cup full or empty? Do you come to your tea as 5.2 grams of Puerh tea harvested by the Menghai factory in 1997 using the 8582 recipe, with slightly larger leaves… or are you empty? Can your cup hold the tea you wish to drink, or has it too become something you've filled with ideas, opinions, questions or comments? And can we really enjoy the aroma, the flavor or the comfort of a cup of fine tea when we've made of it but another topic in our libraries?

There is enough to think about, worry about and debate in our lives without making the times set aside for our relaxation into something serious. Instead, let tea be just leaves and water. Approach it with an empty mind, ready to learn from the liquor itself rather than from a book on tea processing, history or other trivia. Some of that is fun and we're all curious; it can also be useful when purchasing tea, for knowing about tea production makes one an aware consumer. However, now that the tea is before us, let us wash away all the intellectual traps, whether about tea, Zen, spirituality, the Way we should live or even the Way we should drink tea… just leaves and water.

There aren't any questions about yourself to which you don't already have the answers. There is nothing about the tea you need to know which isn't taught by the liquor itself. There is no need to record the moment with an internal dialogue—no need to describe the tea. There is just leaves and water.

When asked how to practice Zen, the master responded: "Drop all opinions!"

Don't approach tea as the scholar in this cup-story. Don't come to the mountain hermitage of your tea space with a lot of questions in the form of words. Instead, sit down before your cup of tea with a clear, relaxed mind—open to any wisdom it brews. This is, in fact, how the Zen adept approaches life: as if each moment was the master, and there was something to learn from every blade of grass.

The tea sessions, like any words that could describe them, are just "fingers pointing at the moon". They are a basket to convey something deeper. And that is why Japanese tea masters have often called tea books, tearooms and even their disciples by names like: "forgotten Basket (*Bosen*)" or "Abandoned Basket (*Hosen*)". After the basket carries something, it is abandoned.

Dump out your cup. Throw out all you have learned about meditation, tea or the Way. There is no need to understand tea when we can let the tea understand us. A simple, empty cup or bowl resting on the table as it awaits tea is the perfect symbol of the Zen mind: always beginning, always humble and waiting.

Lao Tzu often said that it was the spaces between a house's walls that made it useful, the hollow part of a pitcher that held the water; and, we may add, it is the freedom of the empty cup that makes it beautiful: I am that cup, humble and indiscriminate. The cup doesn't object. It holds great and mediocre tea alike. It also remains untainted after the tea is drunk. It is filled with a tea for some time and then releases it without a trace. Thoughts also pass through my mind, like tea through this cup; and let them also leave no traces to taint my future tea sessions. Let my mind also spend the majority of its time empty, so that when the tea is finally poured it will be fresh and new, unaffected by any cups I've drunk in the past. The tea I had before doesn't matter—only this cup! The moments that have gone or are yet to come also are not in this cup here before me. Without judgment, plain and unadorned wisdom is poured into me, emptied again, poured, emptied… If your mind is too full, empty it; and if it's empty, fill it. That is the natural and skillful use of a cup: empty… full… empty… full…

Your cup is now empty and awaiting the tea that will soon be poured, filling you with wisdom and Truth more palpable and real than any concept of an experience can ever be. Each sip is pure, unadulterated living wisdom and monumental presence, here and now. This is your life, it isn't elsewhere and there is no need to think about it, rationalize it or analyze it—just drink it!

You devas should know that all such forms are taught by buddhas according to the ways of the world and not according to their inexpressible meaning.
—The Buddha—

The Second Cup

Chop Wood, Carry Water

Have a cup

When Yun was the third son to be born to a wealthy merchant family in Nanking. Unlike his ambitious brothers he was patient, quiet and had a peaceful temperament. From an early age, the local abbot had watched the boy and suggested to the father that he become a novice. The idea was suitable to Chen's father because he was, after all, the third son and there was great merit in giving a son to the temple. It was suitable to Chen as well, because his older brothers picked on him, and because he found the temple serene and the monks friendly. Without much ado, Chen left the World of Dust and became the novice "Wu De".

As he grew older, Wu De took a genuine interest in life at the temple and the teachings of his elders. He began spending more and more time meditating. When he would ask his teacher for the meaning of the teachings, his master would just send him to chop firewood and gather water for tea. Wu De couldn't understand why his teacher always avoided his questions. He wondered if it was because he came from a wealthy family, who had donated largely to the temple's upkeep.

Wu De grew up and was eventually ordained. He continued meditating, though each passing moon only seemed to rise with more questions. He was looking for answers; they needn't be profound, but answers nonetheless.

"Am I to view the statue in the temple as part of my mind?"

"Gather some nice, clean charcoal and bring the water for tea."

Other mornings, he would think that today would be the day his teacher would transmit the teaching to him. He would be too excited to meditate properly, coming to his teacher at dawn to ask, "Why do we meditate at all if we're already enlightened?"

"There is an especially nice piece of charcoal I saw on the top of the basket last night. Grab it on your way to get some water and we'll have some splendid tea," replied the master.

Soon, Wu De's craving for the transmission of higher wisdom made the trail that led away from the temple gate more and more inviting. When he finally asked permission to travel, his master happily conceded. Wu De didn't need to pack; he simply said goodbye to his fellow monks and walked down the trail.

Eventually, Wu De reached a remote mountain, where he'd learned from monks and laymen that there was an Immortal residing. Surely, this enlightened being would have the answers he sought.

Wu De walked peacefully through the fir trees, past a few streams and around crags, enjoying the fresh, clean air. He wasn't really sure what it was he wished to ask the wise man when he found him, only that he knew there was some secret mystery he was missing, some truth eluding him just around the next bend.

Just as the trees were beginning to thin out, Wu De rounded a corner and came upon a woodcutter chopping wood, perhaps to carry back to town. He humbly asked the man if he had seen any sign of the Immortal who resided on this mountain. The woodcutter smiled and said that he did indeed know about the enlightened being, and that if Wu De would travel through the next valley he might come across his house. Wu De thanked him and continued on. After some time, he came to the cottage; and while it was obvious that someone lived there, it was empty. Wu De decided to wait outside, figuring that the sage had gone out somewhere. He waited and waited, for three days and nights. He began to wonder if perhaps the Immortal had left. Giving up, he decided to return to the town.

When he arrived at the local temple, he told the abbot that he had indeed found the Immortal's house, but he hadn't been home and hadn't come back.

"Amazing, nonetheless!", exclaimed the abbot. "So many people have scoured that mountain looking for the sage, and you are the only one I know of that has ever found his house. How did you get there?"

"A kind woodcutter gave me directions," replied Wu De.

The abbot stroked his beard, "What did this woodcutter look like?" Wu De described him as yay-high, with bright black eyes and a long, black beard with strands of white. The abbot fell off his cushion laughing.

"What is it?"

"My dear friend" he patted Wu De's knee when he got his chuckles under control, "that was no woodcutter." Wu De realized what had happened.

The next day he returned to the valley, sure that the house would be gone. He smiled, surprised to find the cottage just as it had been, only smoking from the hole in the roof. He entered and the sage offered him tea. Wu De apologized for the previous day and the sage waived his sorrys away with his hand. Afterwards, Wu De asked the old master to initiate him: guide him down the Path. "I wish to practice the way that you do, and become immortal myself. Teach me your meditation and I will practice sincerely."

"My teaching is simple," began the wise old man, and as he spoke Wu De could see the depth behind his eyes, trembling through each word: "In fact you saw it yesterday: I chop wood and gather water for tea. Here, have a bowl." He slid a wooden bowl across the table to Wu De, and as he sipped the dark liquor he found that the elliptical rim of the warped bowl mirrored his own journey.

While the next pot is steeping

Zen is the absence of all religion. And yet, Zen is also the culmination of the religious experience. The Zen mind is a celebration of every single ordinary moment of our lives—everywhere we go and everything we do is our practice, our religion. Through mindfulness, devotion and adoration, even the simplest act is purified and made extraordinary. The Zen mind is a holy mind—a buddha-mind that contains the world within it: every slant of sunlight, every blade of grass, every breath is an awakening of wisdom and a celebration of life.

The ancient tea sages knew that if we were to live a life with this kind of Zen mind, tea could never be rushed. It had to be adored. For that reason, they would walk miles to get the best water and then heat it on the purest of charcoal. Even the act of gathering the water and wood was itself a meditation, before the tea ever began. The pots, cups and utensils are there as tools to promote *Samadhi*—one-pointed mind. When the mind is fully awakened in *Samadhi*, there really is no mind at all. Mindfully, the utensils are picked up and put down. Without any extraneous thought, and without tension, there is a precise awareness that arises out of such undivided space. This is our true nature.

So much of our lives is rushed, racing on towards our own death. We wish to drive, fly and communicate faster. We want the morning of work to end so that we can have lunch; after lunch, we want the afternoon to be over so that we can go home. We are always racing away from the present.

Don't let your own time for relaxation—the precious few hours you have to do what it is you want—become rushed as well. We drink tea in our free time, for enjoyment. Take the time to adore your tea. Like the great tea sages of the past, even in this modern day we can still gather our own water. It may not come from the best mountain spring in China, but perhaps there is a river, a stream, or even a lake or well nearby from which you can gather your water. Remember that it will be boiled anyway. And the walk through Nature will do us good, as a time for reflection. If there's no clean water near you, you can first sigh and smile at the humanity of it all, and then find another way to bring some *Samadhi* to your water, like keeping it in a precious jar. It really all does start with the water—remember that.

Many of us may also choose to use hardwood charcoal. Without an on/off knob, charcoal requires skill and devotion. The Japanese have always considered the laying of charcoal an essential aspect of the tea ceremony, and the guests will always compliment the host on the way he or she performs this. Not only does this make an art of our tea, but it brings mindfulness, adoration and celebration to the simple act of boiling water. In using pure fire and water we've gathered ourselves, we aren't being snobby, trying to create more refined flavors of tea. Sometimes we want to impose self-centered thoughts on our tea, or judge the tea of others—analyzing the preparation, the skill, the tea and teaware, breaking it all down into adjectives, grades and levels of quality. In that way, our tea absconds its mountain home and with forlorn grace shrugs and enters the city gates to live amongst the Dust of the World.

Lu Yu and the great tea sages drank most of their tea alone, save for the moon reflected in their cups and the whooshing grove of mystic bamboos that recited for them poems older than the river. They weren't trying to impress. Lu Yu wasn't suggesting that we seek out the best water and the pinnacle of fire—that we devote our lives to the creation of the perfect tea—in order to show it off to someone. Many of these ancient tea sages walked hundreds of miles (yes hundreds) to get the best water for their tea, and this wasn't pretension—they just loved tea. They knew that in walking that mountain trail to the spring, in learning the art of laying charcoal, we are learning to make more than a bowl of tea—that what we are in fact creating is a state of mind, a Zen mind. Their devotion was intense, and they would travel through snow and rain to find tea bushes. Shouldn't our devotion to this, our only life be likewise ordained?

With a bit of reverence for the ordinary, daily acts of chopping wood and gathering water, drinking tea and loving it as a celebration of life—a relaxation of the ego—everything begins to make sense in a reposed kind of way. You can sigh and lean back in contention, knowing that the moment is complete. And yet, how mindful you'll be when you've a fire to tend—when the water took you an hour to gather! Lao Tzu said the Way is a returning, for in a circle the highest is near the beginning. We often travel far to find a different vantage to look upon the simplicity we began with: birds always return to their nest, just as all things eventually come home to their origin. In Zen, too, we return to that softer beginning before our socialization and education—the time when water was just water and leaves just leaves.

In the truest sense, we could go to the store and just buy a bottle of water with awareness, mindful. We could use an electric burner and mindfully turn the knob. However, most of us aren't there yet. We aren't monks with hours to spend sweeping the lawn, until each pendulum-motion of the broom slows to an eternity. Instead, we curiously must practice having the time to brush aside the nearby moments, past and future, and make room on the cluttered desks of our lives—room for a vase of flowers and a cup of tea. It is possible to brew tea in some "Two Minute Machine" and have it be Zen, glowing with perspicacity and wisdom. But that would depend on the mind of the one using that machine, and if you are at that level we can only bow with the deepest respect. For the rest of us, a trip to the mountains to gather water or a long journey to find some tea leaves in the forest or mountains will do us good.

We'll need to practice infusing our lives with Zen. We need to work on celebrating the ordinary. And what better place to start than with our tea? Why not take a walk to a nearby river one Sunday morning, quietly and mindfully gathering a jug of water for that week's tea? Why not try laying charcoal in a brazier, taking the time to properly enjoy the water as it heats up? The word "Chanoyu" means just that: "hot water for tea". Try slowing down and sitting in meditation as the water heats up. Really listen to its song as it stretches out into silence, breathe and prepare the calm composure that will soon stir to life as the ceremony begins. The whole purpose of the tea ceremony, formal or not, is to heat up some water for tea; and if we can bring a bit of reverence to that act, imagine how much brighter that bowl, cup or mug of tea will shine.

So much of what we do in our lives is sloppy and improper. Why not brew our tea properly? Why not make it with an attention to detail, love for the water we gathered ourselves, the fire we tended and the focused, loving attention to every single detail that goes into its completion—culminating in that amazing sip that we have brought together, like the Immortal alchemists mixing the Elixir of Life on some ancient Chinese mountain. That's *Samadhi*, composed in tea.

One of Rikyu's "Four Virtues of Tea" was Reverence. The others were Tranquility, Purity and Harmony. In finding a way to revere the tea and the moment of drinking it, we complete the tea and it completes us. That's the difference between a tea *ceremony* and a Styrofoam cup with a tea bag. It's not a ceremony because it is religious, "Buddhist" or involves some kind of chanting in old languages between sips. Tea is ceremonious because we make it sacred: we uplift it. And if tea, why not life?

Nothing is wanting or lacking, because we've done everything properly. The water has been drawn mindfully, the charcoal laid with skill and devotion. What is left then, but to listen to the 'soughing of the wind through the pines' as the water is heated? When you make room for an ordinary moment to shine with reverence, awareness and completion, it becomes an enlightened moment. It becomes Zen.

The Way of Tea—
Follow it, and ever deeper it leads on;
Like the endless fields of Musashi,
Where the moon is most lucid,
Its depths draw us onwards.

—Rikkansai—

The Third Cup
Shake Off the Dust —Morning Glory

Have a cup

The Daimyo of several prefectures, and regent to the *Tenno*, Lord Toyotomi Hideyoshi himself, presided over his annual Morning Glory viewing party. The guests included three other Daimyos and lords, several high-class merchants and a few of his retainers. After an elegant meal, the regent led the party outside to his garden to see the Morning Glories. His gardeners, of course, spared no expense, and the scenery around the Jurakudai palace was exquisite, with lovely walkways, bonsai trees, a stream and pallets of Morning Glories planted everywhere.

The hyperactive Daimyo bounced along ahead of his guests, pointing out blossoms he found particularly amazing, sniffing others and then rushing off. He asked each guest what they thought repeatedly, to the point of what would have been rude had he not been the host and such a powerful lord. Hideyoshi was a blunt man, though, and eventually he cornered his retainer Sokyu, asking him: "Sokyu, tell me plainly and truly, is this not the most magnificent bloom of Morning Glories you've ever seen?" Sokyu knew that if he was not completely honest, the sharp-witted lord would see it in his eyes, and so he hesitated.

"Come now," said the Daimyo, patting his shoulder, "I don't mind. Tell us whose garden is better so that we may go there before the season is over. Or if it was a past garden you saw, more magnificent than mine, please tell us how we might improve this arrangement."

Sokyu bowed repeatedly, before stammering "M-m-my lord, this year Rikyu's garden is full of the most amazing Morning Glories I have ever seen. Th-they are truly large and white—beyond belief! Not only are they large, my lord, there are so many of them… more than I've ever seen in one place."

"Rikyu?!" He stroked his goatee. "Well, we shall see… perhaps you're right." He summoned a servant and sent him off to inform Rikyu that the lord was coming for tea first thing the next morning: "Tell him a bold claim has been made. Tell him that I've heard that his Morning Glories are the most beautiful in the land, and if it is true, his lord is most eager to see them." As the servant hurried off, Hideyoshi turned to his guests: "In fact", he began energetically, "I think I shan't be able to sleep a wink tonight!" Without any more interest in his own garden, he led the guests inside for some refreshments.

Sure enough, Hideyoshi was up before dawn, dressed and racing out the door towards Rikyu's house—full of excitement and anticipation in equal measure. He strode so fast his samurai had to jog to keep up. He rushed through the streets to Rikyu's house, pushing open the gate to the tea garden forcefully, ignoring the mindful way that his teacher had taught him, and strode boldly into the garden with a huge smile, expecting to be greeted by a rush of vibrant white. Instead, the garden was completely bare. Every single blossom had been plucked… not a single Morning Glory in sight!

Hideyoshi was agape. He stared around in shock. He could see the Morning Glory plants clearly, green and vibrant, but not a blossom anywhere. As this sunk in, the Daimyo grew angrier and angrier until he was boiling. He stomped down the path of stones, pausing ever so briefly to splash water on his face—only because he was Japanese and forms and rituals were always upheld, even in fury—though the meaning was lost, beading and rolling off his fuming anger. He threw off his sandals and burst through the small entrance into the tearoom, a tirade of curses for his teacher hovering near his lips. As he crawled through, he looked up, allowing his irate eyes to grow accustomed to the dimness as he searched for the source of this outrage. His teacher hadn't entered yet, but it didn't matter, for as Hideyoshi looked up he saw it…

…there in the alcove, presented in the most beautiful Ming Dynasty vase he'd ever seen, was one, single absolutely perfect Morning Glory blossom—the most beautiful he'd ever seen!

While the next pot is steeping

We must learn to approach our tea by letting go of all the turmoil of the World. The stress of our jobs, our families, and most importantly our opinions—even our desires and dreams are left behind. We clean ourselves of the World of Dust and enter a different world altogether, a world of peace—a world of Zen. There is a great peace in this truth-exploration we call "Zen"—a letting-go and relaxation just through the rickety, old gate—but don't get confused by all the clean beauty as you enter into the garden: Zen is no fantasy play land, la-la blossoms scattered around a carefree paradise. Zen is a living, breathing embrace of this Reality, consciously: a personal exploration of that which is actual. It is true that in this clarification the greens and reds come alive as they have never before, but there is a stark sobriety to the Truth as well; for don't the trees wither? Doesn't each spring's bloom drop, fluttering groundwards? And for that reason, Zen resembles an art more than it does a religion. If you're busy landscaping a temple-garden of theology, dogma, rights and rituals and are losing touch with this your *only* life—in all its joy and pain—it's time to prune the bushes.

Sen No Rikyu clipped all the blossoms as we must cut all Worldly ties before entering the tea space. Hideyoshi had come seeking abundance and Rikyu taught him that only with an inner emptiness can one truly appreciate a blossom—and the same can be said of tea. Though we have the best of tea and teaware, if our minds are tainted as we approach the tea space, we will only find fault in even the best of tea. There is no abundance here, for each blossoming tea session is perfect, and only the mind that contains it can be imperfect. The mind has fault, not the tea. We must learn how to appreciate a single blossom before we can admire a garden, a single moment of life before we can live enlightened.

The master needs but one blossom to express everything Zen about this world, whereas the clumsy need a whole bouquet. Similarly, the master of martial arts needs only one strike—precise and powerful—while the beginner must swing wildly. When the mind is centered, we can truly express Nature and ourselves in a way that moves people, showing them their own inner abundance. The real source of any and all abundance is within you, as is everything you could ever desire, obtain and then let go of—not of the outer garden, but the inner tearoom. And that is why, in true mastery, all skill is forgotten. It took eons of patient evolution to reach that one blossom, though its creation was effortless.

In Japan one follows a "dewy path (*roji*)" to the tearoom, entering through a crude wooden or bamboo gate. This is meant to symbolize a portal to another state of consciousness. We leave behind all our quotidian affairs, and make the tea space a complete dimension of its own. You can see through these rickety, old gates. They aren't meant to keep people out, but to remind us that from this point on, we are in a sacred space apart from the ordinary humdrum of material existence. The very word "roji" means "the ground that is disclosed/uncovered/illuminated". And it isn't rocks and grass that one follows as one walks down some very real rocks and grass. If not the soil, what ground is then illuminated?

There is usually a water basin halfway down the *roji* that everyone stops at to wash their hands and face, with cool water in the warm months and warm water in the winter. The idea is that we are washing clean the Dust of the World. In ancient times, cities were literally dusty, and this quickly became an important spiritual metaphor—so that renouncing the World for the life of a hermit in the mountains was called "Shaking off the Dust." We clean our face and hands of all Worldly business, entering the tea space refreshed, clean and open. The Chinese also clean all the teaware—cups, pitchers, teapot, etc.—before beginning to brew tea *gong fu*, which means with artistic presence, with mastery. The cleaning of the teaware symbolizes this same sentiment, a washing off of one's cares. It is more than just a hygienic gesture; it is an expression of the purity of the tea space.

We may not have a *roji* leading to our tea space, or a stone water basin with a bamboo dipper, but we can still practice the essence of cleaning ourselves before we drink tea; and the meaning behind the motion is of far more importance anyway. One way I have found to achieve this at home is to bring your guests white washcloths gently soaked in warm or cool water, depending on the season. I use wooden tongs, and like a flight attendant on an airplane or a waitress in a nice restaurant, I serve each of my guests a moist towel. It humbles me and helps everyone to feel clean and refreshed before tea. And whether they recognize it or not, it is also a token action, intimating purity and a leaving behind of all quotidian concerns. As the pores of their skin open, and the face and hands feel fresh, clean and relaxed, their consciousness naturally finds repose and awareness as well.

I also wash off all the teaware thoroughly before and after drinking tea. All the cares of the World are thus cleaned off; and at the end of our tea, we wash off even the tea we've just drunk and all the wisdom it inculcated. There is no attachment in Zen, even to Zen itself.

A student once asked Master Zhao Zhou the meaning of Zen. "Have you had your rice?", he replied.

"Yes, sir."

"Then go wash your bowl!"

As the student walked off to wash his bowl, he achieved enlightenment (*satori*). He understood that he had just been given a great teaching—about life, meditation and also the meaning of Zen. So go wash your teaware!

There is plenty of time for our Worldly life, our professional or family drama, our past or our plans. Let the tea space be free of all that. Turn off your cell phone before even approaching your tea. Wear some comfortable clothes. Clean off your face, washing the Dust away. Then wash each bowl, each pot; because it is sanitary and healthy; and because here, in this space, all our cares are also cleaned so that we're free to find our Morning Glory.

In honor of my tea, I shut my wooden gate,
Lest Worldly people intrude,
And donning my silken cap,
Brew and taste alone.

—Lu Tong—

The Fourth Cup

No Distinction

Have a cup

The great Zenji Zhao Zhou was standing by the door with his attendant greeting any who came for the evening meditation. A layman who had heard about these evening sessions had come to try for the first time:

"Welcome, kind sir," said Master Zhao Zhou. "Have you ever been here before?"

"No, I have not. This is my first time, Master."

"Have a cup of tea." Was the reply.

The attendant also bowed, watching his master's every move. Soon, another layman came into the hall. And once again Zhao Zhou said, "Welcome, kind sir. Have you ever been here before?"

"Yes, I have, Master. I come every week."

"Have a cup of tea."

The master's attendant was puzzled by this and asked the master, "Why, when one of the laymen said he had never been here you told him to have a cup of tea, and then when the second said he often comes to meditate you also said 'have a cup of tea' the same?"

"Attendant!" Exclaimed the master.

"Yes, Master?"

"Have a cup of tea."

While the next pot is steeping

The tea space is a place where we leave our egos behind. As we mentioned before, in Japan people wash before entering the tearoom, symbolizing the cleaning off of all Worldly concern—the wiping of the Dust, so to speak. And Japanese tearooms often have a garden outside and a "dewy path (*roji*)" that leads to the tearoom—a gate that represents a portal, an ingress to a different state of consciousness. The most famous tea master, Rikyu, also furthered this trend by incorporating the 'crawling-in entrance (*nijiriguchi*)' through which everyone had to get down on their hands and knees to enter, and the style quickly became popular. The whole ambience of the gate, the path sprinkled with water, the basin to wash and the little door you crawl through is to prop up the ordinary act of drinking tea—promote what is ordinarily extremely profane to sacredness. You might misunderstand this and think that the experience is a head-trip—a kind of escapism. But the idea is to show what a bit of reverence can do for the most ordinary activity: second only to breathing is drinking.

Even today, the best tearooms or teahouses are the ones that comfort us instantly. We go inside and feel relaxed, serene and at ease. This well-being allows us to spend time with friends, or make new ones, in a space that is free of ego, or any other materialistic matters. We can sit back, take a breather and simply be ourselves. Without any pretension, all the qualities we like or don't like in ourselves, the world or others are left behind; and we're free to achieve true repose. Even when we converse, it is in a more relaxed manner and ideas slide off us without importance. In such a pot, *kensho* is free to unfurl and release its essence.

Zhao Zhou told all the visitors to have a cup of tea because it doesn't matter who they are or where they've come from. When they come in here—into the tea space—they are the same: Egoless. One is reminded of the Indian custom of greeting and parting, in which one places one's hands together and says, "Namaste", which means: "I honor that place in you where, when you are resting in yours and I am resting in mine, we are one." It means that in here, as you quietly sip your tea and I sip mine, there is no name, status or need for discussion of who we are in the World, where we've come from or where we're bound to afterwards. Like our shoes, we leave our egos at the door. Lu Yu also often suggested that in the repose found within the brewing and drinking of tea, we are free to *be* Nature—to commune with the world and achieve unity, wisdom and a sense of the Tao.

Zhao Zhou also viewed the newcomer and the one who came often as one and the same, suggesting that there is no attainment here. The wisdom of tea is direct and simple, drunk in silence and understood by all. As you sip the tea and it courses through you, warming your body, there can be no higher or lower understanding. You can't say the child doesn't understand what he is drinking, for in drinking it he is experiencing it and nothing could possibly hinder that. We can never achieve a greater intimacy with the world than when we take it into our bodies and make it a part of our physical selves.

When the attendant tries to make of tea something intellectual, the master sends him off to be quiet and drink a cup himself. Zhao Zhou loved saying, "Have a cup of tea." He often answered questions in this way, meaning that we should take the focus from ideas, concepts and boggy mind stuff and return to this world—living and breathing: tap the table, touch the cup; it's real! It is too easy for us to get all tangled up in our isms and schisms—theologies, philosophies, and opinions (Zen or otherwise)—and then we start living a head-trip, out of touch with this life. The only real and meaningful truth in our fantasizing is the recognition of its nature as such. In these instances, the master sees there's not enough tea in our Zen: Have a cup of tea!

Sometimes the "no-mind" often referred to in Zen is confused for some kind of idiocy, where empty-headed zombies float around in "meditations". What it really means is have a cup of Truth—Reality as it is, concretely; not as an abstract, like the way in which ideas and ologies live only in the mind—that if you are truly aware as your mind thinks its thoughts, there is space behind and within the thoughts, containing them. And that awareness is the capacity to think itself: the space in which any given thought arises. It is not that we stop the mind, but rather stop falling into the muck of the thoughts themselves, rolling around in the contents of our mind. And when a question is witty, haughty or insincere—perhaps a jab to provoke argument—it's better to recognize this tendency of the mind to get entwined in the contents of our thoughts and return to the moment: Have a cup of tea.

Zhao Zhou himself traveled most of his life, only becoming a resident monk at the ripe old age of eighty. As he traveled he painstakingly kept a vow that he would bow and beg for instruction from anyone, anywhere or anything that had wisdom—even if it were but a village boy—and offer instruction to any that sought it, whether sage or tree. There is peace in such indistinctness—when we stop categorizing and compartmentalizing everything and just have a cup of tea.

Relax, free yourself of all social constriction. Tea gatherings in Japan were the one place people of very different classes could mingle, and many lords and samurai were so attracted to *Chanoyu* because it was the only place they could be free of all the stringent mores that governed every aspect of their professional and personal relationships. In such a formal society, it was cathartic to slip out of one's tight, crisp clothes every once in a while. And though we aren't living in ancient Japan, we still have rules governing our conduct—professional and personal—social status and other constrictions on our behavior. In the tea space, we are free to let go of all that and be ourselves, to follow our intuition and act spontaneously and comfortably. There is only hot water for leaves here.

The tea space is for sharing together in a comfortable space. There is no need to impress or show off. It doesn't matter where you've come from or are going to. We are both here to "have a cup of tea!" The great thing about tea is that it is affected as much by the mind of the participants as it is by the tea's quality, the teaware, brewing methodology, etc. It is, after all, the mind that wills the hand to lift the kettle, the mind that wills it to pour—smoothly, gently or rough and splashing—and so much of our state of mind is transmitted through the tea we brew and serve to others. But the best tea isn't made by the active, thinking voice in the head. You have to shut the commentary off. The best tea comes from *no-mind*, which means the spaces between the thoughts—the gaps that are, each one, infinite and eternal buddha-nature.

Zen cannot be analyzed. There are no manuals that can live your life for you. You have to *be* this life, not think about it. And even when you are thinking, you have to *be* that thinking. It is tough for us to wrap our minds around a living philosophy, especially one that is inclusive enough to accept even our intellectual games, using them in *sutras* and *koans*—mostly to direct our attention back onto ourselves and our personal exploration—to see the Truth in our reflective games: that the eye cannot see itself, the tongue cannot taste itself, nor the mirror reflect itself. These words "Have a cup of tea" are as useful as any sign—any finger pointing at the moon. But the real answer is neither in nor out, pointer nor the pointed at. It isn't rational at all. When you ask what enlightenment is, the answer is a cup of tea; what is the Path—a cup of tea; how do I find Zen—a cup of tea. Without talking and without remaining silent, right now—Quick!—show me your Zen… One answer is this cup of tea. Another is…

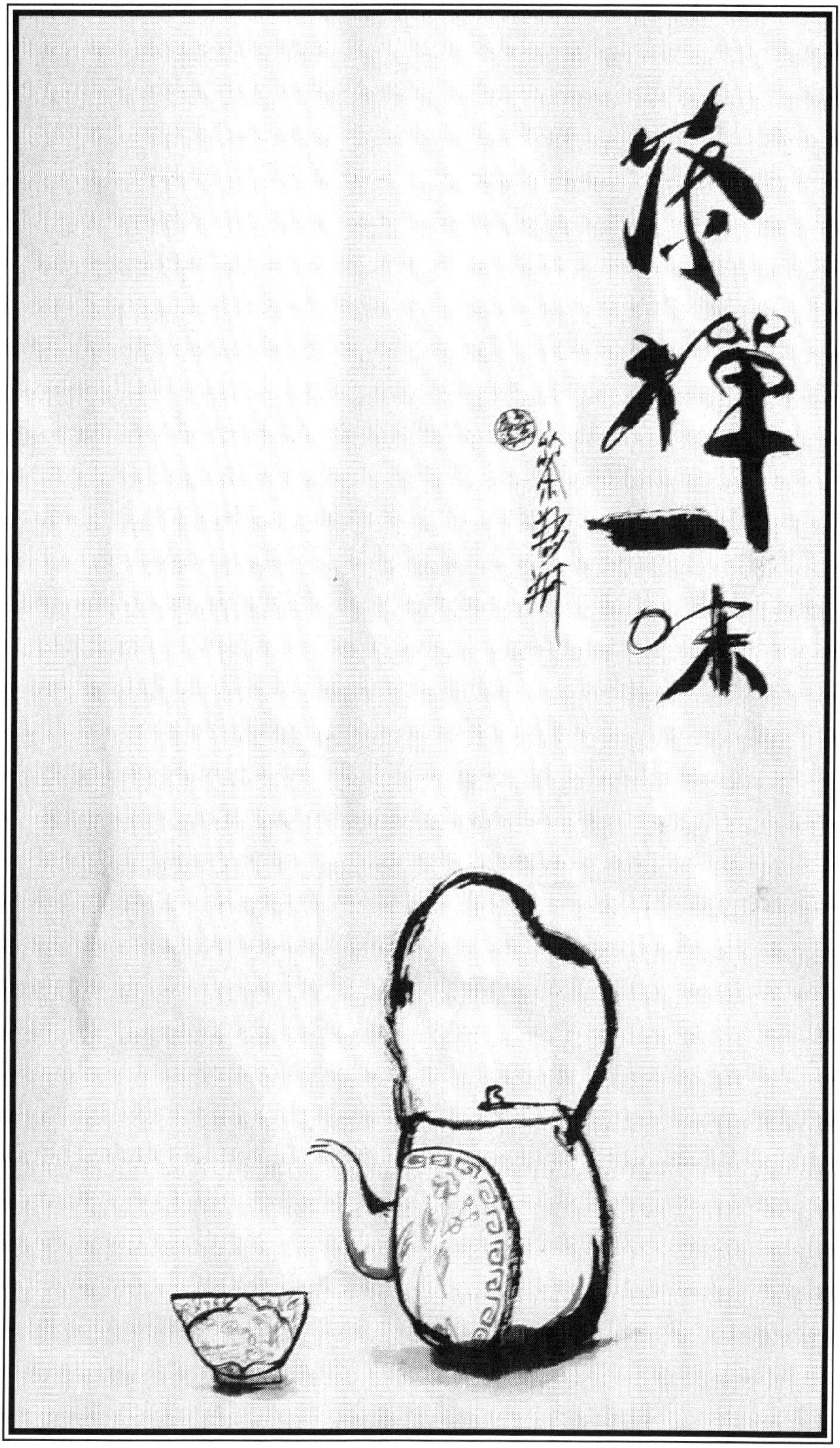

茶禅一味

The Fifth Cup
Tranquilitea

Have a cup

Two great Zenjis met one afternoon at a temple they both went to occasionally, finding relaxation in the nice gardens there. They were both renown for their wisdom, though Chokei was the more famous of the two—celebrated throughout the realm for his ability to elucidate the inner essence of any of the *sutras*. When he lectured, monks and laymen both would travel from far to hear him, amazed at his ability to recite from the vast scrolls at leisure and his ability to connect various teachings in new and insightful ways. Chokei thought the meeting fortunate, as he had often heard his students speak highly of Hofuku. He thought that this would be an opportunity to speak on the *sutras* with an equal, perhaps shedding some useful light on his own practice.

The two men walked quietly to the small bamboo hut and sat down in the shade. Hofuku was smiling. The sun was shining and the weather was balanced perfectly between spring and summer. "We are well met," he said. "To share such a day is one of life's greatest joys." Chokei agreed and offered Hofuku the seat of honor, which he took without any hesitation or pretension. Hofuku began heating the water for tea and they sat listening to the water boil for some time, watching the great mountains move along at their ancient pace. When the water was ready, Chokei thought it a nice time to begin their discussion.

"Hofuku, even if an *arhant* were to have some evil desires, I still say the Tathagata's words were one. A Tathagata has words, but never are they dualistic."

Hofuku ladled some water into the *yuzamashi* to cool. He smiled, "What you say is insightful, but your viewpoint is not perfect." He then steeped the tea. Chokei was overjoyed that the master might offer him a new perspective. He grinned, "What is your understanding of the Tathagata's words?", he politely asked.

Hofuku poured the green tea and offered a bowl to Chokei.

"This", he answered.

While the next pot is steeping

In this modern age, so many of us have turned our backs on silence; and yet without silence and stillness it is impossible for any living thing to be healthy. Were are force-fed the illusion that technology will one day solve all our problems, including the ones created by technology itself, and that the answers to life are to be had in the accumulation of more tools— tools to clean our tools' tools in fact. Actually, all we need is a bit of stillness amidst all this activity: some windless calm within the storm. Nature always balances a time for vigor with a time for rest, and we ignore Her at our peril. The ancients knew this well, and even busy government officials actively cultivated pure leisure through art—often a tea garden near their house. But the periods of quiet must flow together with the times for activity, as different harmonies of the same song. Zen meditation is not a drug to bliss out from the world; tea is not escapism.

Silence is the greatest ally of the Zen mind. At first we practice developing outer quiet, becoming comfortable with a silent room and a quiet cup of tea. As our tea drinking quiets down, other activities begin to follow suit, and soon enough we find true silence: inner silence. Many Zen masters have said that it is easy to be quiet when the body is still, but a truer expression of Zen is the silence found within action. The Chinese sages called this "wu wei" or "effortless action"—action without an actor, in other words.

We boil the water, brew and then drink the tea, but we do it silently; and not so much in the sense that we aren't talking, but that our minds are silent. Then, even when working, talking or eating we can be at rest. The ancient Taoists often compared this state to a deep lake: though the surface is rippled by the winds of change, most of the water is eternally still just beneath the surface.

The greatest gate to pass through on the Way of Tea is also the most important in life and Zen, for they are not two: when tea preparation turns inward a great barrier is breached. We realize that the true source of the calm in tea is within us, and the best tea is prepared from that space. That is "kensho"—illumination of our true self, our very nature. And true skill and art comes from that inner calm, and has nothing to do with intellectual knowledge or technical expertise. Then tea preparation sails a natural current towards stillness. When things in this world are at rest, they naturally clarify—the silt settles, clarifying the water, as the dregs flutter to the bottom of the resting tea bowl. This process is natural; it requires no effort on our part—in quietude things reconcile to stillness of their own; when distractions are set aside, the mind quiets and the breath slows down—the world then becomes clearer and sharper.

Learning to cultivate inner and outer silence is an essential part of most all spiritual traditions the world over, and tea can be a great ally in this, making the process enjoyable. They say that there is already quietness inherent in tea, just as the original Mind is also quiet. The tea wants us to be quiet, and rewards us with subtler flavors, hidden aromas and an experience of our living energy, called "Qi" in Chinese, when we still ourselves and approach it quietly.

All the books on tea won't prepare it or drink it for you. Collecting information and then discussing, analyzing and criticizing it only distances you from the moment, and the enjoyment of a free, relaxed atmosphere of unruffled peace. If you ask a master painter to explain their masterpiece, they can't. There is no intellectualizing experience without distancing yourself from it. Similarly, it would be extremely difficult for most of us to chit chat about Worldly matters or philosophize while meditating. We can't fully drink a tea, enjoying its flavor, aroma and Qi while at the same time talking, and that includes all internal dialogue as well. Recording your tea for some future discussion in the form of a ledger of notes, a blog or other kind of journal is just as distracting, and the wisdom of the moment is lost. It is very difficult for most of us to turn off the internal voice—words describing what we're experiencing—long enough to really have a drink, to be or live any moment of our transitory lives.

The great Zen master Huang Po would never answer questions that forced him to recognize concepts or ideas of possession, instead answering with silence—a reserve that was often interpreted by those arguing with him to mean an acceptance of defeat. Perhaps in a way it was a surrender of the intellectual arena, though some of his students would walk away feeling as if the master had alluded to something more: to the idea that Truth is above and beyond all words or the concepts they symbolize, found only in the profound silence that blankets the highest peaks.

In these stories when the masters are saying, "Have a cup of tea!", they are really saying, "Have a cup of Wisdom!" In other words, we come in and set our egos down with our shoes. We then quietly have a drink of ourselves: we breathe and silently sip, noticing the warmth of the cup, the smell of the tea, its flavors and sensations in the mouth, the way it warms our chest and throat, and the oncoming Qi. This is also Lu Yu's "loving attention" suggested all throughout his book, the *Classics of Tea* (*Cha Ching*)—in the way we adore the water and fire and perfect their preparation, for example. We participate in our tea, becoming it fully. There is no need for me to take notes and describe what I taste, for you can't ever understand anyway. You need to experience your cup as I drink mine. Any accord to be had will be in that space alone.

Some of the absolute best tea sessions I have ever had were with monks who knew nothing about tea processing, history or even how the tea we were drinking got from the farm to their pot. And some of the worst sessions, on the other hand, were with great tea scholars who, even though they were drinking very rare tea the monk could never afford, ruined the session by bickering and debating, analyzing and criticizing every facet of the tea, from its flavors to its history—meanwhile, the tea was unfortunately left unappreciated. Isn't it the same with Zen? Even a cursory survey of Zen literature and the dialogue between all the "schools" and "traditions" demonstrates the old Taoist saying that "those who speak don't know, and those who know don't speak" (present company included). The best Zen isn't debated or analyzed, for tea and Zen are one flavor in the end.

All the facts in the world won't help you make a better cup of tea. "Trivia is trivial!", my teacher often says. Tea isn't brewed with an intellectual understanding of processing, history or other factoids. Zen and tea are of the same flavor because tea is brewed best by the heart and soul. My master doesn't make better tea because he knows more; he makes better tea because he *is* more.

The art and Way of tea is in the soul, and past to present as tea spread throughout Asia and beyond, masters have always known this love and passion. Lu Yu adored tea, covering it with only the best of water prepared on the pinnacle of fire. He brewed it with unequalled attention, making sure he found the perfect moonlit grove to enjoy his mystical "three cups". In this drink, I'm quieted—necessarily, lest I choke trying to speak—and beyond that, may my mind quiet as well, re-establishing the much needed communication between Man and Nature, so prevalent in Lu Yu's time and so often neglected in our own.

We just drink tea, enjoying it and our companions as well as ourselves (if there are any). Hofuku's secret isn't difficult, in other words. There are no libraries to sift or tests to pass; beginner and adept alike "Have a cup of tea!" That is his true understanding of the *sutras*—a quiet beyond even the idea of 'quietness'.

Let us instead of talking here, drink of the wisdom of tea, which is the wisdom of Zen, and save any other words we've left to say for another cup-story… As the steam rises, and we're all silenced, perhaps sighing and leaning back to relax—smiles spreading across our faces—there is a very real sense in which we are united in the Tao, one in tea. That is the sharing of the day master Hofuku was alluding to; that is the cup that expresses his understanding of Zen. And we may drink of it now, just as Chokei did so long ago, for the same cup is staring up at you now, beckoning you into the stillness just beneath its rippled surface.

Ever so silently I steal into my chambers.
Deserted.
Empty and barren too is the grand hall.
Waiting.
Patient for a man who'll never return.
Resigned, I turn to my tea.

—Wang Wei—

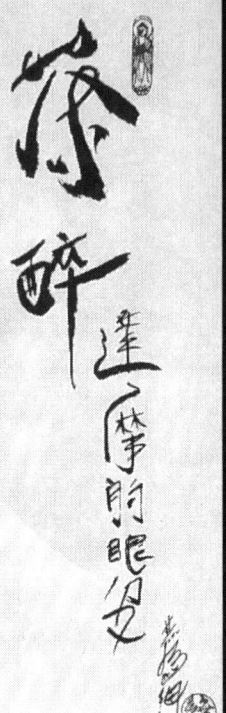

茶醉 達摩的眼皮

The Sixth Cup
The Wind Soughing the Pines

Have a cup ☕

In finally finding the old master, the student bowed and asked to be allowed to study Zen. The master passed him a bowl of tea in acquiescence.

Each day they rose before dawn and climbed the lonely trail through the pines behind the temple. They would sit for some time in the pre-dawn hush. Only when the sun had crossed the back of the hill and sprinkled its splendor upon the evergreen boughs would the old master draw water from the ancient spring there—an honor not for the novice hand. Then, just as his master had done before him, he would bow before the old tea bush at the crest of the hill, long ago named "Bearded Immortal", and politely ask for a small offering. The student would watch most carefully at that point, for his master had said that the secret way of processing the tea was all and everything in this lineage, and everything the temple stood for. When it was ready, the master would return to his seat and bow to the tea and teaware once more. The preparation was simple, yet with a grace that betrayed years of mastery, if you looked closely at the weathered hands that is.

Sometimes, when they were finished, the student was allowed a question or two, though the answer sometimes took him months to grasp. One such morning, years after he had come to these distant hills, he asked the old sage, "Where is the gateway to enter Zen?"

The old master paused, as he always did—as if listening for the answer. And this time, he did indeed cock his ear up as though hearing some bird language sages such as he had once known. The student followed his example.

"Don't you hear it?", the master whispered: "The wind soughing the pines."

There was no wind that day, and the student heard nothing. His face slackened in disappointment. Noticing, the master said, "If you don't understand Zen, at least understand your breath." The student then closed his eyes and observed the touch of his breath as it came and went through his nostrils, and in that way was calmed—forgetting his question.

Over time, the gateway to Zen became the only unopened door in his practice. Most of their life was, therefore, held in routine, and peacefully so. But every few months the student would again ask where the "doorless gate" was; and always the answer was the same: "the wind soughing the pines." Sometimes, the wind actually would sing its way through the ever-green boughs, and the student and master would both smile in glee. But when the moment passed, the student somehow knew that wasn't it. He was still looking, albeit patiently. In the meantime, he'd heard enough times for his master's admonishments to ring out unspoken in his head: "then understand your breath!" And he'd close his eyes and focus on his breathing once more.

Some years later, the old Zenji couldn't climb the hill without the arm of his student. One such morning, the student was surprised to find that when the old master reached the hilltop, he sat in the student's seat and asked him to prepare the tea that day. He had never done this, but had watched for so long that it had all become second-nature. He gathered the water with just the same gesture he had seen his master using, rolling the gourd over into the kettle. He noticed that his own hands had also weathered and creviced, and in the spring water saw reflected silver threads embroidering his once black beard. His master joined him in prayer before the old Bearded Immortal, and together they roasted and dried the tea in the ancient way.

He sat in his master's seat by the old stone table and rest the kettle upon the coals. Holding it was like holding the hand of your father at homecoming from a long journey—the worn, wooden handle seemingly carved to mold to his own hand. He relaxed, closed his eyes and waited for the water to boil. He now understood his breath enough to settle into it, while at the same time listening attentively for the sound of the water awakening in the kettle.

And then it happened!

From out the silence of the mountain, the kettle began to sing and the student heard the "wind soughing the pines." He was a student no more; he'd crossed the gate. A Zen smile brightened his face and he opened his eyes to share this with his master. Surely his master would see his enlightenment. But to his great surprise, his old master was gone—vanished!

Instead, a young monk walked over, sat down and bowed. He asked to be allowed to study Zen.

While the next pot is steeping

Zen and tea are the same because Zen and life are the same. The world around you, all you see and hear, *is* the sacred. And you needn't go to the beauty of the pines to see it—the same sound is in your manmade kettle. The passage to Zen is without door; and what, imagine, is a gate without its doors or lintels on the side? Such a portal would be endless and embrace your whole life. You have but to walk through it, this very moment. And through the gate, the heart opens and Zen becomes who you are. Each moment is then religious, and the most ordinary sip of daily tea is a hallowed ceremony.

There is an old story of a Zen master and his student who were meditating deep in the forest. The disciple paused and asked his master where the gateway to Zen lay. "Listen," said the master, "Do you hear that distant stream?" The novice cocked his neck and strained: sure enough, just beyond the wind's arpeggio of leaf-bells and past the birdsong there was the sibilant drone of a distant river. When the master saw that his student had indeed heard the riversong, he said: "Enter Zen through there." The student then asked, "What would you have said if I hadn't heard the stream, Master?" The old monk grinned, "Enter Zen through there!"

Oftentimes we confuse the whirlwind of experience and situations around us for who we are. And yet our "true face" watches from the center of this, unmovable. Do you identify with the experience or the one who experiences? Is it not your *ability* to perceive that defines you? Are you not the consciousness that reads these words, rather than the words themselves? If so, you know then that the one who hears, not the sound, is your Zen; and the sound itself is but the trail that leads up the hill, past the pines, to the gate.

Searching for "Zen" in beliefs, traditions or meditation postures, we pass by Reality as it is in this moment. We want a special sound, not this sound—heavenly music perhaps. We want visionary sights, not cars and buildings. But Zen is the one who sees and hears, not the sounds and sights; and when we rest in that space, all that unfolds within it is sacred. Seeing and then *being* our true selves is "kensho".

Are you denying your life now because there is a hint of fulfillment in the future? If so, you don't understand Zen. You'd better work on understanding your breath. Otherwise, even if your dreamed-of future arises and all the circumstances of your life fall into place just as you had imagined, you'd just rush past that experience as you did this one and all the others between—on your way to somewhere else. Are you on your way to somewhere else? Won't you pause for a moment? Please, come in. Take off your shoes. Have a cup of tea.

There really is nowhere else for us to be, and nothing else to be done. Take a break. Have a cup of tea. If you have nothing to do, then nothing remains undone. Only those who have identified completely with activity, rather than the one who acts, are busy getting this and that done; and when you're busy trying to get things done there is always much more that is left undone.

Zen masters have always meant to communicate this identification with pure consciousness, able to contain any sound or sight, smell or touch. Do you get it? It isn't really all that complicated: there is you and then there is what you experience; there is an awareness—an ability to hear or the "sense of hearing" and then there is the sound. But you can't just understand the idea; it's misguided. You can argue with it, finding flaws. You can compare it to other Zen books and lectures and point out discrepancies. You have to really listen. You have to get in the water, not just understand what swimming is about. The tea is in the preparation, in other words. Make some tea. Zen really is that simple.

On the other hand, it is sometimes possible for words to point this Way out. After all, what are words but symbols we see or sounds we hear—air passing through our vocal chords, passing through the air and vibrating the eardrums? Other times, however, words get all bunched up in the head and clog the mind up. Attached to meanings and concepts, we then roll in thoughts and lose our ground: the awareness capable of thought—the one who thinks.

It is a paradox that these moments lost in activity, of the world or of the mind, are also just a part of Reality as it is. Still, there is some unmentionable quality missing from the life lived completely within the content, and a sparkle in the eyes of the one who is in constant contact with her true self—the one with *kensho*—that is missing from the eyes bent upon Worldly sights.

Some Zen masters spoke in absurdities, and the students would then ponder them until their minds got so tangled they fell apart. The words weren't ever important, they'd then realize. The pith of Zen is passed on nonverbally—usually by living around the master for years, until the water of his life steeps into yours and such little things as the soft way he smoothes his robe, or perhaps turns over the gourd of water, speak volumes more than any scripture ever could. My master has transmitted his Zen to me through drinking tea together, and that time is more valuable than any particular teaching I can remember.

Hundreds of years ago, as today, so much could be shared between master and student when they drank tea together, especially in quiet. If it is done skillfully or with love, a kiss can tell a lover more than a thousand love letters.

In tea, there are a thousand opportunities to pass through the gateless gate to Zen. As your water warms up, relax and breathe deeply. Close your eyes. Understand your breath, noticing the way it touches your nostrils. As you calm down, try to rest in an awakened space, listening quietly and patiently for the first stirring of the kettle. Let it happen naturally. There is no need to do anything, not even wait. It will boil when it wants to, and the sound will be your invitation—a chance for *kensho* to arise. Do you hear the wind soughing the pines?

If asked
The essence of Cha Tao,
Say it's the sound
Of windblown pines
In a painting.
                    —Sen Sotan—

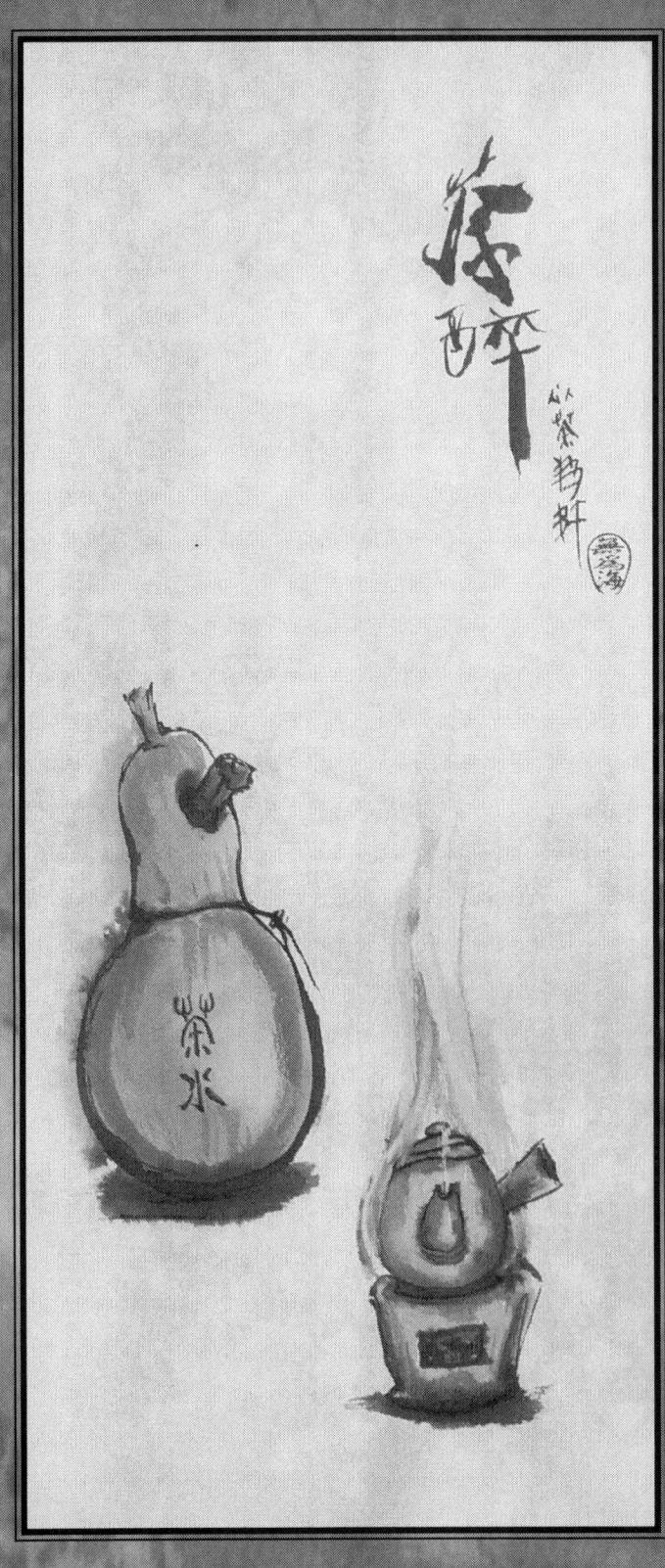

The Seventh Cup
Remember the Soul, Forget the Bowl

Have a cup

The great tea master Murata Juko was once invited to share tea with some samurai in the nearby mountains where they could also view the spring blossoms. The nobles asked master Juko to prepare the tea, though they had organized the gathering and brought the teaware.

The bowl was several centuries old. It was a masterpiece brought over from China by Zen monks. Next to it, were two of the most valuable pieces of teaware in all of Japan: a tea scoop and a *chaire*, or tea container. The scoop was lacquered wood, inlaid with gold and silver. It had once been used by an emperor. The *chaire* was of antique porcelain, also painted with red and highlighted with gold leaf. All three treasures had been brought by different samurai, and each was worth a fortune in gold.

Several of the samurai commented on how amazing it was to have three of the greatest treasures in the history of teaware together for the first time. The effect was startling, indeed. With the mountain air and blossomed trees forming a glorious backdrop, it was "perfect"—they all unanimously agreed.

"There is nothing missing from a moment such as this!"

"Just look at this teaware!"

"Nothing could be more perfect. Isn't it so?", one samurai asked the master.

"Almost", was the humble reply.

"*Almost…* what could be done to make a more beautiful tea arrangement than this!", exclaimed the samurai.

The master didn't wish to be impolite and dismissed the conversation with a smile. But the samurai wouldn't let it go, and their attitude was friendly. They cheered and clapped, demanding that Master Juko show them how perfection was bettered.

The old man bowed and with a careful attention, replaced the lacquer tea scoop into its silk bag, which then was returned to its wooden box. He put it aside with the other teaware that was not to be used. He then got up and walked over to a small grove of bamboo that bordered the trail they had followed to get there and plucked a small stalk. On the way back, he removed the stems from the stalk and broke one end in half, forming a very rough trough. This he placed next to the bowl as tea scoop.

While the next pot is steeping

Renunciation has ever been central to Buddhist practice. The ancients called city life the "World of Dust" and leaving it behind was "Shaking off the Dust." Since roads weren't paved in old cities, the bustle did stir up quite a bit of dust, and the metaphor was therefore perfect. The dust stains our clothes and gets in the eyes, preventing us from seeing things as they really are. We need a bit of clarity—some time in the cleaner mountains to brush off the dust we've accumulated living in the World, as well as an unclouded view of our lives to see them as they are.

But true renunciation doesn't really have anything to do with the objects you own. In truth, none of us "own" anything, not even our bodies. The atoms that circulate through you and I were here before us, and will remain long after we're gone. They are borrowed. Similarly, there are more molecules in a single bowl of tea than there are bowls of water in all the oceans of the vast Earth, so molecules we drink and absorb have also flowed through countless other beings—like Master Juko and the Buddha himself.

St. John of the Cross wrote that the monks in his monastery were often more attached to their single possession, a rosary, than some kings were to their palaces. Sometimes kings are indeed unattached. Knowing that they can replace anything in the palace, they can be generous and unconcerned about it all. Is the attachment to an old, cracked bowl any different than that felt for a golden statue?

Attachment to an object means that we have invested it with a part of our self, and view its loss as a personal diminishment. Actually, no object can in any way enhance or reduce who you are. It doesn't matter how cheap or expensive, how big or small—nor how many people and contracts there are establishing that a house, car, bowl or painting is "yours". In the end, your relationship to that object will dissolve. And whether you recognize it or not, the truth that it was never yours to begin with will be demonstrated. It takes Zen eyes to see this. You have to wash off a bit of the dust.

This doesn't mean giving away all your things necessarily serves any purpose either. Though its nice to live in the mountains, where the air is clean, the Tao prevails in the dusty city as well. An aversion to nice things, just because they are valuable is also contrary to the true meaning of renunciation. Sen No Rikyu, the greatest tea master of Japan, helped his lord, Hideyoshi, construct a tearoom that was completely gilded in gold for a visit by the emperor. In fact, it was at that time that he was ordained and received the name "Rikyu", which history went on to remember him by, since lay people weren't allowed to be in the emperor's presence and Hideyoshi needed Rikyu there. Later, another tea master named Sokyu criticized Hideyoshi's golden tearoom, saying that he didn't understand tea or Zen. Rikyu, however, defended his lord and turned the tables on Sokyu in a rather insightful way: he said that all the golden walls, panels and even golden teaware were indeed extravagant; "And yet, my tea sessions in that splendorous room have all been transcendent." Sokyu was too focused on the value of the gold to appreciate the beauty. To a lord like Hideyoshi, the amount of gold used in the construction of that tearoom was minimal and not extravagant at all. Rejecting it based on the value the human mind has placed on gold, rather than evaluating it as it was, came from the same kind of dusty mind that would crave to possess it just because it was gold. Some people reduce the tearoom to gold they are greedy to own, while others reduce it to gold in order to denounce it as "extravagant".

The Buddha taught that craving and aversion are a hair's breath apart. Master Juko recognized the balance of a true Zen aesthetic, and life. Without ever owning a treasure, it is possible for someone to justify their lack with an apology based on Buddhist renunciation. In other words, true renunciation is in the heart; and the one who understands things as they really are (kensho) has already let go of all possessions. But this does not mean that such a master cannot appreciate beauty. That is important to remember. Turning away from an object because of its cost means you are still focused on the delusions of mind-made value, and aren't able to see the object as it really is: beautiful to the human sentiment. A master can also recognize, appreciate and delight in beauty and craftsmanship, she just doesn't wish to possess it—or perhaps you could say she isn't deluded by the idea that she could actually possess anything, most especially beauty.

If you ask the novice monk for his only possession—a beautiful tea bowl perhaps—he will feel conflict, giving it to you because that is what his beliefs say he should do, though his heart tells him to keep it. The master will laugh, seeing through your desire. He will keep the bowl, as long as it remains useful to him. If you are unattached, giving away your bowl doesn't improve your relationship to the things around you. The master would only give away the bowl if it were truly of benefit to do so, perhaps helping one with no bowl. Again, it is the heart that matters.

On the other hand, teaware can become an academic debate in which libraries are written and discussed, time is spent arguing aesthetics, clay composition or other details, but as such the essence of the teaware itself is lost. In Japan, many critics of the tea ceremony often rebuked tea people (*Chajin*) for that very reason, saying that while the ceremony was meant to inculcate simplicity, renunciation and the purification/beautification of the spirit, actual tea people often just ran around buying expensive teaware and chatting or arguing about its many nuances. The very word "Chanoyu" literally means "water for tea"; and the simpler we keep it—water and leaves—the purer our intention. The real treasure of the tea ceremony isn't the pots or cups, no matter how much you paid for them—the real treasure is the true self, Nature's vessel, which is divine and therefore of limitless value.

Master Rikyu once attended a tea party where several rich samurai and lords were showing each other expensive teaware and antiques and discussing how much they were worth. One of the lords then noticed that throughout the evening Rikyu had remained silent. He asked the master for his opinion. Rikyu humbly asked to be excused. The samurai, however, pressed him to offer some insight. "You all seem to have missed the point," he began, "the value of a piece of teaware is reflected in the tea it makes and the state of mind it brings about, not whether it is expensive or cheap, new or old." Perhaps none of the lords understood the admonishment, though they surely responded politely.

The ancients saw that it was natural for the human mind to crave for possessions, expanding the sense of self to include the objects around us. In defiance of that habit, they taught poverty. Still, the same danger remains, for the ego can use the fact that it owns "nothing" to enhance itself, and the monastic robes thereby become as much of a status symbol as the rich woman's fur coat. Juko's insight is that true poverty need not be taught, or practiced. It is inherent. Neither the pauper nor the prince truly possesses anything. Since we already, inherently cannot ever possibly own a single thing, we have but to recognize this fact and embrace our natural state as it is—naked we come, naked we go.

As we travel through this life, we must interact with objects all the time. Some are beautiful, others naturally lead to revulsion. *Chajin* naturally love and appreciate teaware, flower arrangements and other art—sensitivity to such beauty is an essential aspect on the Way of Tea. But we mustn't allow that second thought, after the appreciation and heartfelt grace, to mar our veneration with a desire to own, based on an illusory self and a deluded idea that we could possibly own anything at all. Zen means seeing things as they are—*kensho*. We must observe ourselves, not blindly grasp or repudiate any thing just because it is a thing.

Our ancestors recognized the individuality and spirit in objects and treated them with reverence. Very little was ever discarded. And when an object is seen as having its own life, it's easier to let it go its own way when the time comes. My master says our teapots are friends and teachers that come into our lives to show us things, then move on to other places and friendships. We must accept them with grace, as much as we part with them in poise.

It is our relationship to the world that is important, and the most skillful approach is the rustic tea scoop in equilibrium to the treasured bowl. Both are more beautiful and poignant next to each other than they are when apart—the elegance is defined by the simplicity, and vice versa. Too much refinery is gaudy and too much forced, man-made simplicity is contrived and often suppresses inner turmoil. The Zen mind delights in the magic of an antique tea bowl, molded by some ancient master's hands and crowned with golden highlight, without wishing to possess it; and treasures the simple bamboo stalk, deftly turned into a tea scoop by one or two forthright alterations.

If you have one teapot
And can brew your tea in it
That will do quite well.
How much does he lack himself
Who must have a lot of things?

       —Attributed to Sen No Rikyu—

The Eighth Cup
Leaves and Water

Have a cup

The novice Enshu wished to study tea, finding the flavor of Zen more in the cup than in the Zendo, especially the evening lectures. His own tea, at dawn in his small cell, had taught him more of his only life than all the sermons and retreats he'd ever attended.

Enshu heard that a great master of Zen and tea named Sen No Rikyu was teaching in distant Kyoto. He shed his robes, abandoned the tonsure, donned a coarse peasant robe and set out to travel the great distance on foot. Finally, he reached the outskirts of the city, where the master lived. He waited outside the gate until dawn. When the master came forth, he bowed and asked to be taken as a disciple. Rikyu left him there and walked down the street. In the evening, when the master returned, Enshu was still sitting there, despite the crisp autumn wind. Rikyu let him in and offered him some tea.

As the months passed, Enshu learned to gather water at dawn, when it sparkled with the Yang energy of the sun. He learned to arrange the charcoal to the perfect temperature so it would burn for hours underneath intricately layered patterns of ash; and to whisk the tea until the aroma filled the room and pacified the air. Rikyu taught him slowly, rarely saying a word. He would simply draw his student's attention to what he was doing, often with just a glance. Enshu was a good student. His years in the monastery had served him well. But he was young. Somehow he felt that he hadn't yet grasped the Tao of tea.

One day, as they were tending the garden and Rikyu was showing him how to pluck the flowers for the day's arrangement in the tea room, Enshu asked: "Master, I traveled the breadth of the empire to study this Cha Tao. What is the true essence of tea? What is the highest truth as expressed in this tea ceremony?"

"Ahhh…", said the old master, raising his eyebrows in a way that had Enshu up on the balls of his feet in anticipation. Surely some esoteric secret was about to be transmitted.

"The very essence of Cha Dao," Rikyu continued, "is this:

> Gather water,
> raise the charcoal,
> boil the water,
> steep the tea.
> Then,
> drink it."

Rikyu nodded to himself, smiled and returned to his gardening.

"But... but..." protested Enshu, "That cannot be it. I traveled all this way to learn that! I already knew that before I left. It is too simple!"

Rikyu tsked, "Enshu, my son, the day that you can do as I've just said, I will walk across the entire empire to your home, rest my head at your feet and with all the devotion I can muster call you master til the end of my days."

While the next pot is steeping

In all cultures, art has been used to express spiritual truths not easily captured in words. Symbols and paintings, poetry, music and myth often point more clearly towards the experiences and living truth that is the core of the religious life. Sometimes, also, the presence of the right art is itself enough to uplift us.

The Zen tradition offered the world its own unique insight into the creative process, beyond just expression or communication. The Zen adept also recognizes in art a direct transmission of experience as well as a bold expression of truth—like the poem spontaneously composed as an outpouring of an enlightening experience: the Buddha's "lion roar". Beyond this, however, Zen also approaches the artistic life *itself* as an aspect of art—not just the process that leads to artistic creation, but a form of art in and of itself. Rather than focusing exclusively on the results, no matter what they express or communicate, the life of the Zen artist is in itself another kind of art, expressing its own truths.

The Zen master uses the creative process as meditation. He seeks to purify this creativity—removing any trace of the egoic mind—so that the poetry, painting, calligraphy or pottery happens of itself, as if spontaneously sprouting from Nature. Not only does this art then communicate more directly to that same space which is beyond understanding or not-understanding, but it transforms the artist herself.

In true art, there is space that surrounds the composition—where the mind has let go of the voice that all-too-often imposes itself upon the clarity of our true, boundless minds, confining them in silted ponds when they should be oceanic. The suchness of the moment is then channeled into an art that others can interact with much more directly than other mediums of communication. The artist's whole life leads up to that moment of creation, and there is no real clearly defined boundary. The tangible form that is the art, in Zen, comes from a purified, empty mind; and therefore expresses a bit of the emptiness out of which it has arisen.

Emptying the mind and allowing such creative forces to gather enough momentum to take form isn't just about the actual time spent practicing one's art; it encompasses every aspect of life. The calligraphy master thus admonishes his students that if they want to brush the perfect scroll, they must simply perfect themselves and then paint naturally. The purified mind is like Nature itself: majestic and inspiring in all its creations.

The art of tea is also expressed through these principals. Master Joo often told his students that very little of Cha Tao has to do with the actual preparation of tea, or anything to do with the tearoom. If your life is in turmoil, a few moments of breathing won't purify your tea. If you make a habit of internal noise, your art will be noisy. We develop purity, clarity and tranquility in ourselves, using tea preparation as the Worldly axis around which our Zen orbits—gathering momentum, so that when a fellow traveler stops by we can communicate this space directly. And what could possibly be more direct than a mind distilled into liquor, and drunk by another?

"Show your Zen without words and without silence!", is the master's challenge. And it isn't about the answer: words—even absurd, like "mountain lilies in the breeze"—ink cursorily flung with abandon, or tea. It doesn't matter how you answer; only what space the answer was drawn out of, just as the water's purity depends on which spring, river or well it was drawn from. And there is no fooling in this, for the master recognizes wit. He knows how to look, which you need to learn as well—if you're to see the Zen in any art, because that's just it: Zen isn't something you can see. It's how you see—with the Buddha's eyes.

Arts like calligraphy, poetry, landscape painting, tea and even swordsmanship have all been very powerful expressions of Zen as it is shared between people, as well as Zen as it is lived. The artist's life culminates in the Zen mind, and then communicates it to others. The ancients said, "speak what cannot be practiced, and practice what cannot be spoken." The actual artwork, then, is analogous to what can be spoken, and the life and mind out of which it arose are that which cannot. And that is a big part of why Zen is so much more expressible through art than it is through logic, discourse or study. In the moment, here and now—with these unique beings—expression can happen in its own way. Each person of Zen will have his own way of showing it, which certain people may relate to, feel and understand. Thus, I share my experience, strength and hope in this book just as the bird shares his in birdsong.

You needn't call yourself a Zen master to develop in tea. Just learn to prepare tea, and the process will purify you if you allow it to. The skill needed to prepare tea properly requires a serene mind, and as you drink tea each day you will become more and more sensitive to which areas of your life are out of tune with the melody the tea is composing. But to do this is not as easy as it sounds. Master Rikyu isn't condescending—he's serious: It will take a lifetime to simply brew some tea!

As you drink tea, you begin to love it; and as you love it, you begin to live it. A life of tea then steeps into the other aspects of who you are, and your diet, exercise and other routines slowly incorporate themselves into the creative process. And unlike other art forms, the connection to the Way of Tea is much more powerfully consummated, for the creation itself is consumed—losing all meaning and returning once again to your body and daily life: A Zen circle, called an "Enshu".

The highest level is also the simplest. Tea is "daily life Zen", as simple as eating when you are hungry and drinking when you're thirsty. The highest expression of life is the one that can be just so. The best tea is prepared in that way also. You are the water-gathering; you are the boiling and steeping—and after some time, when art and life consummate, you realize that you are drinking Zen.

Clear in color and refined in taste.
Faintly aromatic with a slight bitterness.

—Lu Xun—

The Ninth Cup
Thunder —Tempest in a Teacup

Have a cup

Two young monks were on a pilgrimage, as their ilk was wont to do when in youth they still believed in searching for that which cannot be found. After a long retreat in the mountains, they were passing through a small village. As they walked, they discussed their individual attainments during the long period of silence, occasionally debating the meanings in reference to various scriptures they'd read or sermons they'd heard. Seeing a small teashop at the end of the village, they decided to warm themselves before continuing onwards.

The shop was very simple inside: a single, old wooden table with a bench and a few stools around it, a bamboo alcove and an old scroll with a single word brushed powerfully across it: "All". The shop was very clean, if plain. The proprietor was an old man, and judging by the small size and emptiness of the place, he lived alone. Still, something unspeakable sparkled in his eyes—that playful charm that only glimmers in eyes that have seen enough of this world to know.

The two monks sat down and the old man prepared them some bowls of tea. They continued their conversation about states of consciousness, now turning to the various masters they had so far encountered on this voyage and their degree of enlightenment. The old man smiled, pouring them some dark liquor that swirled with steam as it flowed from a worn pot older than any of the deep wrinkles creasing his brow. He also poured another for the simple village woman who sat meditatively on one of the corner stools listening to all the monks said.

The two monks drank their bowls and their spirits calmed. The importance they had moments ago felt for the points they had been arguing drifted away like the steam; and other things came into focus, like the way the sun's rays slanted into the dim room, taking shape and substance, or the glowing, now-golden grains in the old wooden table those rays fell upon.

The old man poured a second bowl. As soon as the pot was put back down, the old village woman clucked her tongue and the two monks glanced over. They noticed her simple clothes, worn by labor, and yet how beautiful and unpretentious was her smile.

"Masters and enlightenments", she chuckled and glanced down at the steaming bowl of liquor before her, sighing, "Let the Fully Enlightened One, Master of the Ten-Thousand Things, second to none, Buddha of All Ages and Realms, Warden of the Cosmos and Endless Tao—Let this one, and this one alone take the next sip, in all honesty—for Kuan Yin's sake!"

The two monks paused in askance. Was she crazy, their eyes seemed to wonder. Who could possibly take such a sip! They glanced at their tea, at each other and waited for the woman.

The old woman grinned, lifted her bowl and drained it in a single draught. She rose from her seat, wiped her mouth on her sleeve, sighed in contention and left two agape monks where that sat in the shop.

While the next pot is steeping

There is a tradition, grown in Buddhism and steeped in Taoism, which has come to be called "Zen". But is it this tradition that is passed on from master to student, down through the ages to our own? If not, then what is transmitted? Don't you see how difficult it becomes to even say "Zen"? It makes you want to set the book down, bite your tongue and reach for the kettle. If you say Zen is conveyed, what is it that is handed on by the master? Surely not a robe and bowl? Furthermore, by who is it passed on and to whom? On the other hand, if you say nothing is passed on in the learning of Zen, why did Mahakashyapa smile in understanding when the Buddha held up the flower on Vulture Peak? Why did Bodhidharma bother coming to China? And what did his robe and bowl, handed down to each successive patriarch represent?

Must we then be left adrift, wondering if Zen is some otherworldly mystery only reachable by the greatest of saints? Most definitely not! The same Truth hovering between that mythological flower-smile is here right now in this very place where you are! The meaning of the bowl and robe— Bodhidharma's marrow—is steaming before you now! And you—Yes, you!—can drink of it this very day. There's no need to travel the globe searching for a master; no need to study difficult, old books, learn ancient tongue-twisted languages or jump through esoteric rings towards some inner sanctum. It's sitting right in front of you now—in that very cup! Isn't this what Bodhidharma brought from India to China? And if not, what?

The ancients repeated again and again that true Zen was beyond all discourse—beyond even the Buddha himself, of whom we are reminded to "kill if we see him coming". The *satori* that reeks of *satori* is not true *satori*, just as the worst *miso* bean paste stinks of *miso*, while the best has no odor. Likewise, a wayfarer can stink of Zen, and a tea practitioner can stink of tea without being a true person of tea. Those who stink of Zen need to drink more tea—a good master would tell them: "Have a cup of tea!" And the tea people (*Chajin*) all hung up on collecting expensive pots, cups and teas they hoard, and don't drink, definitely need to find the Zen in their tea—to them the master also says, "Have a cup of tea!" (maybe with a smack on the side). In defining "Zen", which can only be successfully achieved by actually living and breathing Zen—walking the Path—you ultimately reach the insurmountable cliff wherein the Truth is carved: *to understand the essence of Zen, you must be Zenless.*

The life you are living couldn't be any more real or true than it already is, no matter what ideas or beliefs you impose upon it. You may laugh when this realization really sinks in. A monk once asked Zhao Zhou what happens after all of one's possessions are given up, and the old master exclaimed, "Abandon!"

"I already have nothing!", protested the young monk.

"Well, then, carry around as much of a burden as you like!", was the rejoinder.

The young monk really hadn't yet given up all his possessions, because he was still carrying around Zen, and the philosophy of "abandoning" itself. If you say the word "nothing", then something still remains!

We scramble around, like young novices, traveling around from teacher to teacher and mountain to mountain—searching for an experience of Reality (big R). A master might be saintly, but if we find in her a single flaw—even if it was just a rumor of a flaw that happened decades ago—she is dethroned, and we move on to the next, searching for that supernatural master made of cloud, with a voice of thunder. All the while, that same Reality (again, big R) wasn't changed an iota by our quest. It was, in fact, the space that contained our whole voyage. Any number of teachers and lessons pass us by every single day. In arguing whose teacher or tradition is "real Zen", what is it we can achieve? What satisfaction can be had in proving that a certain teacher or authority is a phony? Aren't we all phonies? Isn't that the very point—the fact of the matter: that all our egoic I-subjects are delusion? My teacher always says: "Even if someone were genuinely ignorant, they'd still be the Buddha of Ignorance, and could at least teach us that much. We should bow in gratitude. And actually, though it's good to bow, who can really say who the ignorant one is?"

When you fold the world into categories of wise or not, pure or impure, Zen or not-Zen, you live amongst the tradition of "Zen Buddhism" only—missing the point on which it was founded. Perhaps we have been too long staring at golden buddhas to see that the village farmer is a thousand times more alive, and thus more powerful. There is an old Sufi saying that "*Allah* is just a sound, and no more powerful than any other sound", which applies just as profoundly to the sound "Chan" or "Zen".

There are many stories that express this truth amongst the vast library of Zen scrolls. The Tang Dynasty master Yao Shan was said to have practiced Buddhism, meditating and reciting *sutras*, observing the precepts painstakingly for many years. One day he reflected that he had to let go of the dharma to find purity, and without hesitation abandoned his tonsure, traveling south to study the Zen that's brewed in tea. A contemporary of his, Master Xuan Chien, is said to have burned the *Diamond Sutra* before retreating within. At the height of winter, when the storm blows the coldest and you're out of fuel, you burn all the Buddhas to stay warm.

Zen masters have always likened the relationship between the wayfarer's struggle with the World (*Samsara*) and her enlightenment (*Nirvana*) to climbing up a forty-foot pole with one's bare hands and then jumping off. It is a great struggle to tame the mind, one exhausting hand after another climbing up the pole. But in the end, we have to jump off. The key to Zen is understanding the perspective the top of the pole offered us—the difference between the one who has never climbed and the one who has just landed, though they both stand firmly on the ground of daily life. *Nirvana* and *Samsara* are one and the same or abysmally apart, depending upon where you happen to be standing—just as all this Zen-talk is either insightful or the paragon of absurdity from different vantages.

Hui Ke, the second patriarch, cut off his arm and handed it to Bodhidharma so that he would teach him to pacify his mind. When Bodhidharma asked him to produce this unsettled mind, Hui Ke said he could not. "There", exclaimed Bodhidharma, "I have pacified your mind!" Though Hui Ke has reached the profound realization that he originally had no mind—that he was a "snowflake in the sun of the Tao"—we cannot discount the years of torment that led him to sacrifice a limb for this truth, searching so painfully and without regard to bodily comfort as all the sages have.

A lot of people theorize Zen, and sometimes even argue traditions—this one over that. Which history is correct? Who was whose teacher and when? Even admitted to the secret *sutra* hall that has the answers to these and all the other facts, would you be different? This is collecting Zen, rather than practicing it—or better yet *being* it!

There is a famous Chinese story of a noble who loved dragons so much he collected everything dragon related: poems, books, paintings, sculptures and ceramics. He spent a fortune and filled his house with dragons. Artists heard about this and came from the corners of the kingdom to craft him dragons of wood, stone and metal. One day, an old dragon came to hear about him and was impressed. He felt honored. Though he rarely ever ventured to the land of mortals, and even less allowed himself to be seen, he decided to pay the noble a visit. He transformed himself into a man and entered the village. He came to the noble's house and was allowed to wait in his rooms, since he was out at that time picking up yet another dragon painting. Alone in the noble's quarters, the dragon transformed back into his natural form. Curling up around the walls, he waited with his great head on his fore-claws. When the noble returned, he heard of the visitor and rushed to see him. When he opened the door, he screamed. Pale and deathly mad, he ran from the house and was never seen again.

Are you searching for spiritual thrills? Does the Zen master in your mind look a certain way? If your teachers have to come with qualifications and pass enlightenment tests, you are walking by thousands of wise men and women everyday, and ordinary situations that offer not only a chance for growth, but the selfsame enlightenment you may think exists only on distant, paradisiacal shores. Self-complacency after some kind of attainment is the greatest obstacle in Zen. "Enlightenment is easy, but maintaining a forthright mind beyond this is difficult", as they say. Are you too proud to humble yourself before the village woman and learn from her? If so, your cup is full and she has nowhere to pour her wisdom.

There was a famous Zenji in Japan named Daio Jomyo who spent twenty years living with beggars under a bridge, even though his enlightenment had been confirmed by his Chinese master, the revered Hsu Tang Chi Yu. His student Daito followed suit, spending some years as a cowherd. How many of us would have walked right by such enlightened men? When you have ideas about what a sage looks like, you bump right into one and either apologize or maybe even scoff—"out of my way!", and on to somewhere else.

Do you think the Zen experience can be qualified? It may be that your life is passing by, and it is trying to teach you all you need to know, and more importantly *be*. "This can't be it!", you demand, and she again sighs and walks on—content that she'll get another chance to try once again to show you your nature some other day. And that is why the real master always shows you her humanity, and in doing so shows you yours as well. The true Zen master is a person in every way, as was the Buddha himself. His humanity is complete, not left behind like used clothes. No part of a human life is ugly to him. He has eradicated all taint, because he no longer sees the distinction between the tainted and pure. If you befriend your enemies, you find lasting peace; whereas defeating them in battle only breeds more warfare.

Similarly, there are experiences to be had in meditation. In ancient India, yogis developed a system of nine "jhanas" or high states of consciousness reached through meditation. Even adept masters rarely passed the sixth. The Buddha studied with many such masters, and reached the peak—the ninth *jhana*—and as such these teachers had nothing else to show him, offering instead to let him remain on as the heir to their communities. He declined, knowing that the bliss found in these high states was temporary, and that the miraculous powers they bestowed—able to read minds or even walk on water—weren't a solution to the dilemma of suffering through this human life. Even if he entered the ninth *jhana* and stayed there for the remainder of his days, his body would diminish, dissolving the mental state that was dependent upon such a body in the first place.

Meditative states are just scenery you pass by on your way. The vistas of your life are ever-changing. Sometimes you can see very far, and clearly so; while other times the tangled jungles of life's matters block out the mountains and sky. But more growth is in such valleys than in the barren peaks. A master once sat before an earnest meditator polishing a brick. When the meditator finally asked him what he was doing, he said he was making a mirror. "You can polish that brick for a million years and it will never become a mirror!" exclaimed the meditator. The master replied: "Similarly, you can polish that ego for a million years and it will never become a buddha!"

The most valuable insight of the Zen tradition—the pinnacle of the religious experience, really—is its own self-consciousness: To be Zen, truly, is to be Zenless. Freed of itself, as a tradition, way, philosophy—let alone the rites or rituals the Buddha himself received so much enmity for casting aside centuries before Zen began—only freed of all this does the unburdened signpost of Zen clearly show the moon of enlightenment. For the ego only ever desires a kind of pseudo-enlightenment, in which it can revel in and exploit its own state of wisdom and sagehood, and thwarts any real progress towards its own dissolution—which is, in point of fact, the realization that the ego as the I-subject never really existed at all, and true sagacity was there all along.

The famous Tang Dynasty monk Niu Tou Fa Jung meditated day and night in a cave amongst the mountains. While aspiring thus, it is said, people came from miles around to bring him offers of food, and even the birds and animals laid flowers and seeds at his doorstep everyday. And yet when Master Fa Jung finally attained the enlightenment he'd sought, the animals and people stopped offering him anything and he had to walk down eighty *li* to the nearest village to beg. Veneration and sagehood were only possible when he was a monk, a "sage"—a "holy man".

This doesn't mean, however, that the master doesn't use the tradition, scriptures or rites. The old village woman probably prays at the temple during festivals, besides drinking the real tea of Zen when she's free—and does so earnestly. She prays the way she drinks tea. Zen means that if you are looking about for certain states of mind or miraculous teachers, take a break and have some tea. The importance of all your arguments then evaporate in the empty, steaming bowl—recently drunk. "What was it I wanted to say?... Never mind," the tea mind replies.

Don't pass by your own divinity. It is in this sip. Don't be afraid to raise the bowl—the way the monks were—for the All is right here flowing through this very moment. Reality is here. Nature is now, in this cup: sun and moonshine, mountain and river cultivated and brewed into this very liquor. Path? How can we travel from here to here? Any and all movement can only be *away* from home!

Even the villager knows that we're all buddhas already. She's connected, not arguing about how to get connected—just tea, nothing more or less. Who is she to challenge Reality? Who are we to argue with the way things are? After all, even our most intrepid fantasies are within minds that are contained by this world and all that is Real. Could anything, anywhere be more real than this bowl of tea?

Drink it. Be this moment, completely and without remainder. Be Zenless, expressing Zen. Without words or silence, you show the reality of your enlightenment by putting the mind aside and taking the next sip. You needn't magical powers to do so, because it is already so incredibly magical that a being with eyes, hands and a mouth on some whirling rock in a corner of endless space is here and now drinking such deliciously aromatic tea! The Reality of that shouts aloud all the enlightenment of a billion buddhas, and beyond. The last line of Master Rikyu's death poem, written moments before he committed ritual suicide, reads: "By my knife, all the buddhas and masters are slain." And the village woman likes this poem. She quips, "By *my* sip of tea all the buddhas and masters are likewise slain!"

A tea tree preaches *sutras*: whispers that summon the wrinkled old hand. He plucks some leaves and dashes them into a bowl, covering it with steaming water: The bowl opens up and swallows the whole universe—the stars and all swirling around as you lift it up to sip. Then you are that one! And going beyond the beyond, the whole thing just wraps itself up neatly—returning from such celestial heights back to an ordinary bowl on the table when you set it down. "Ahhh!" Your quenched thirst sighs.

You *should* wipe your sleeve and leave…
But again you wonder, "What, really and truly, is enlightenment?"

"Three grams of tea."

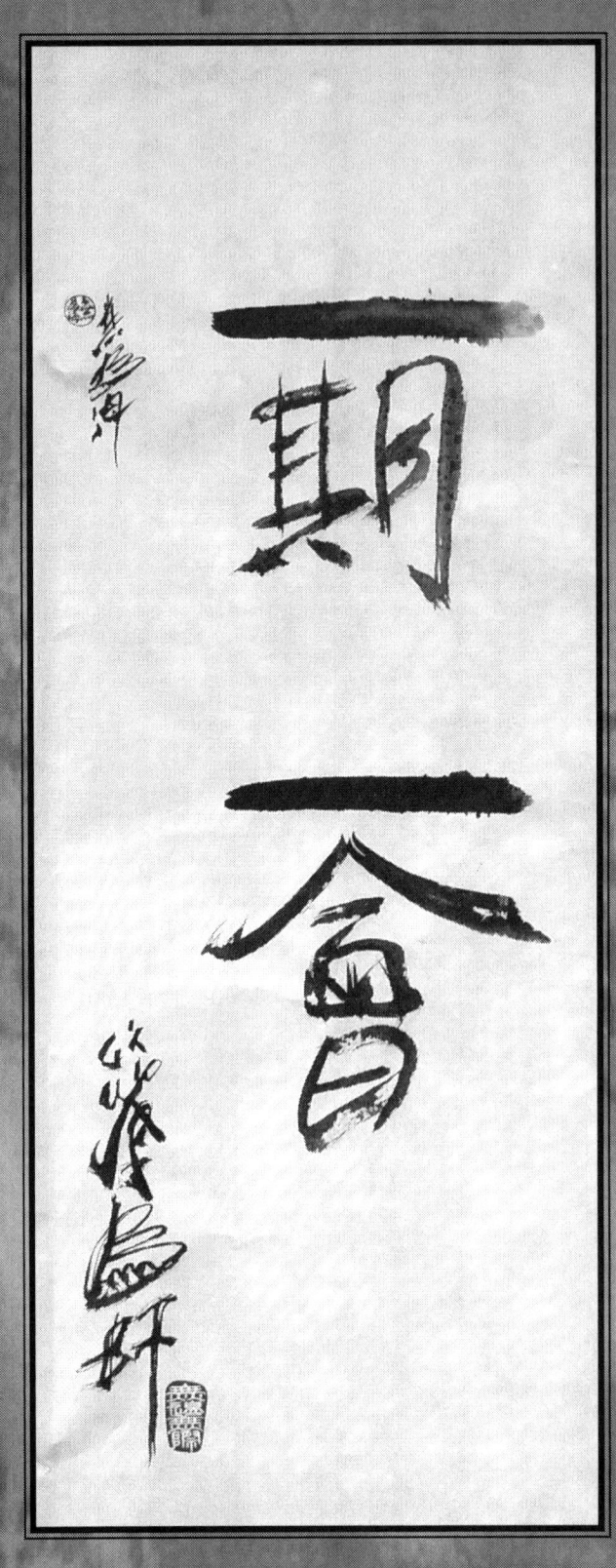

The Tenth Cup
Unannounced

Have a cup

One early spring morning, the master decided to have a walk. The weather had just turned and patches of the greenest grass pierced the remaining clumps of snow in stark contrast. Some intrepid blossoms were exploring the unchartered white emptiness—perhaps as heralds of the pilgrims that would soon follow them en masse. The crisp air, however, was deep and still at rest. It was all enough to fill him up, and he lost track of himself.

Stopping to smell a particularly bold blossom, the old man suddenly realized just how far out of town he had strayed. His student Rinzan lived not far from there, so he decided to pay an unexpected visit—as masters the world over are wont to do.

Rinzan was in his garden, tending to the first tenuous shoots. He too had lovingly caressed a blossom and smelled it, impressed by how fragrant and bold it was amidst the bareness of the fading winter. He'd thought of his master, perhaps at the moment that the other had also stopped to think of him.

When the old man approached, Rinzan put down his tools and bowed. It had been a while, leaving them both standing still—palms still together in respect, as they measured the time in each other's eyes. When his master smiled, Rinzan broke the silence: "Won't you have some tea, master?"

Turning, he casually washed his hands in a nearby bucket, cast off the water and plucked the single yellow blossom he had earlier been admiring. Though that would be the only decoration for such an unannounced tea ceremony, his master had indeed taught him well, for as they entered the small tea hut, the water was already boiling—the kettle singing in greeting. A simple, farmer's rice bowl sat on the floor awaiting them. The alcove, however, was empty. Rinzan took up one of the small meditation cushions and placed it there. He gently rest the blossom at its center, to lord over their tea.

Though there was no other teaware than that crude rice bowl he had planned to drink from himself, Rinzan betrayed no embarrassment before his master. He unpretentiously filled it with tea, covered it with steaming water and whisked it for his master. The tea also was not that used for special occasions. The spring harvest hadn't yet arrived. It was, instead, last year's tea—left over for day-to-day drinking. Rinzan did not offer the bowl in apology, however. With all the reverence of a grand ceremony, celebrating the Full Moon or the New Year, he passed the bowl and with resolution bowed to his teacher.

The old master drank deeply, enjoying the tea slowly and silently. Occasionally, between sips, he would look at Rinzan or the blossom in the alcove. Finally, after an hour or so of silence between them, the tea was finished. The master's eyes moistened: "Alas, I am the master no more." He bowed in full prostration, touching his forehead to the mat, and departed without another word.

While the next pot is steeping

There is an old saying passed on amongst *Chajin*: "ichie go ichi", which means, "one encounter, one chance." It is an affirmation of the power inherent in the present moment, and the mind inseparate from it. There really is no past, save in our memory; and no future either, save in our dreams. There is only this moment, and that is where true Eternity rests—not in an endless future going on and on.

You have this one chance, here and now, to be alive. There is nowhere else to be. Sometimes we compare this world to imaginary ones in which injustices have been addressed and wrongs amended. But such fantasy worlds are incomplete, and the underlying suffering of this one *real* world too easily pierces such idealism, flooding in its own version of the Truth. The underlying dissolution and suffering we all face often causes us to attempt to buffer ourselves by seeking after that which we think is beautiful: we collect things, chase love and romance, lose our minds in fantasy sitcoms, movies and games, cultivate sentiment and dwell on dreams—all in a desperation, seeking to create something lasting. Still, the Truth ever haunts us; and cruelty, violence and the unraveling of everything we do lurks just beyond any veil we hide it under—so much dust lazily swept 'neath the rug. This was the Buddha's first Noble Truth, and the first thing he taught after his enlightenment: that all of life is suffering, and we must recognize and face this fact. He also taught that this suffering could indeed be transcended, but with wisdom and clarity, not more pie-in-the-sky dreaming.

The only real difference between a buddha and the so-called unwise is the delusion, and even it has no real substance. The deluded separate their mind from the world. The Buddha realizes through every particle of his being that his body and mind arose out of this world, the way that tea leaves grow out of a tree. You cannot separate the leaves from the tree, or the tree from the mountain, and so on.

Even if you and I share the same kind of tea a hundred times, and even if we draw our water from the same source and use the same teaware each time as well, each and every session will still be brand new—a unique encounter of energies never before seen in all this vast universe, and never to be repeated again. There is but this one chance.

While it is important to recognize the cycles of Nature, the seasons and stars, the Way is really more of a spiral and we must therefore also pay homage to the ever-changing distinction of this present moment. When you recognize the impermanence and dissolution happening now, you cease postponing your life to some imaginary moment, thinking that you will be fully present at some time in the future when you have worked out some situations that are yet to be what they "should be". There is nothing wrong with goals, but the journey is far more important; and if you aren't present in this step you'll waver from the path and never reach your destination anyway.

The Buddha spoke of impermanence (*annicca*) more than anything else, often testifying to its transformative powers. He quite poetically expressed his entire meditative practice in the ancient word, "sampajanna", which quite poignantly has an etymology that originates in words that mean: "all-consuming fire" as well as "constancy"—ultimately suggesting that our understanding of impermanence must be more than just an intellectual recognition that everything changes, but like the hottest of fires must consume our body and mind—so that we feel every atom, in every corner of our body changing, as well as the thoughts and currents of the mind. And continuing this practice from moment to moment is *sampa-janna*. Like the other great alchemists of history, the Buddha suggested that this sacred fire would be the crucible that turns all our lead-dust into gold.

Sometimes we carve images in our minds of people we've met and places we've been, and then we react to these stone images rather than the living moment itself. It is no wonder many people feel so disassociated from one another. If you haven't seen someone in twenty years and are still reacting to the form he had before—perhaps he was a thief—you are watching an old rerun, not what's on the air now. Maybe that thief transformed into a saint. If suns can explode and transform into planets, which grow life that evolves into people and Zen, then any transformation is possible—possible in this very encounter! In Zen, we wipe away the separation between the mind and the world, becoming fully present. We don't live in the attic, amongst boxes of memorabilia or in the clouds amongst dreams of future worlds, brave or otherwise.

Every moment is unique, every moment is a chance to meet for the first time. But we must be open to it, accepting of Reality no matter what form it takes. That is why Einstein called the Buddha the first great scientist, because he sought to observe things as they are, not impose any fancy upon phenomena. *Dhyana* is seeing and embracing the Truth—Realism. The master in this cup-story saw in his student the same power to spontaneously accept the moment as it is—to be in it, and not try to vainly push it away. When the Truth came knocking at his door unexpectedly, he was open and ready to receive it. What is here and now is the only Reality there is, and struggling with it will only further suffering. Without any of the affectation that surely would have surrounded a planned visit from the master, the student calmly offered what he had. He seized this as an opportunity to share an intimacy with his master not otherwise possible.

There was a Zen abbot who was the paragon of peace and acceptance. One day he was called upon to conduct the funeral rights of a lofty government official who had just passed away. Several wealthy lords and nobles were present at the funeral. During the chanting, he noticed his palms had grown sweaty. As a result, he renounced his position and retired to the mountains to meditate, realizing he was not able to keep his bearing equally amongst all people. We must be present and poised in each and every situation, for it is our one and only chance—our one and only encounter.

Our daily tea is the gateless gate. Use it as an invocation of this very Presence. This sip is your chance to be here in this world, fully alive—and resting in that space is your buddha-nature. You were never more alive than you are now, and no matter how your situation changes in the future, you won't be more alive then either. There is nothing that can possibly be added to or taken away from this universe as it is right now. It is perfect as it is. You could travel the globe searching for the perfect cup of tea, learning all about tea preparation and collecting the best tea and teaware, but in the end the master would ask you to look back and realize—as she has done—that they were all perfect. There was an ancient poet who spent his life searching for the perfect blossom to inspire a verse so deep it would immortalize any that heard it. He devoted his whole life to the art of flower-arranging (*Ikebana*). On his deathbed, in honor of a lifetime of inspiring work, his students brought in a gorgeous arrangement of his favorite flowers. The master looked up and with his dying eye realized that the imperfection had always been in his mind alone. Every blossom was perfect, and that is Immortality!

Imperfection is only mind-made, and is related to the ego's natural tendency to compare this moment to past sensations and future dreams. In a foreign land, the Zen master asked two men who they were and what this place was. They answered that this was *Samsara*, and that one of them was the tallest of the dwarves and the other the shortest of the giants—though they were the same height! One tea costs a few cents for 10 grams and another is very high-quality and costs hundreds of dollars for 10 grams, but scattered in a forest, there's just 20 grams of leaves on the ground. Where then is the tall and short, high and low, beautiful and ugly, perfect and imperfect?

The universe is always inviting you to let go of the separation between the mind and Nature, loosing the illusory distinction that deludes. These leaves and water are another such invitation, but there is only this one chance to be had in this encounter.

In Chinese tea, we practice "Cha Xi", which means arranging the flowers, tea and teaware differently for each session—sometimes with seasonal or celebratory themes in mind. The Japanese tea ceremony has also always done this, calling the seasonal changes "temae". We use decorations, teaware and tea to change the session every time. This is not a pretentious excuse to collect more and more teaware. It should be a beautiful testament of how preciously you value this diamond moment. You can remind yourself by making each session unique, and also communicate this to others as well.

Try allowing this creativity to flow into your tea as well. It is a part of the journey, and the expression of how precious each tea session is. By putting up a scroll painting, some flowers or arranging special teaware you will find that the tea simply tastes better. And the process itself then becomes Zen art, transformative no matter what the result. Spend some time in reflection before cleaning up, but make sure that your tea be like the Tibetan sand paintings, wiped clean as soon as they are formed. The flower is so much more beautiful for its honest transiency—*annicca*.

Tomorrow we are gone. It is a certainty. And yet, there is still this moment of life. It is here and you are amongst it. The great master Dogenzenji said that life and death are completely distinct—life is here and now and death is not; and when death is, life is not. They do not become each other, but exist independently for eternity. Look carefully at the leaves and water before you now. Do you see your chance to be? Do you see how happily Nature has come to view this chance encounter—like long-lost friends meeting unannounced? And now that the master is here—as he/she is for all of us—can you smile and offer your moment without pretension?

When you ask of the dark,
The master shows you the light.
When you ask of the light,
She shows you the dark.
Forgetting shadows and suns,
The world rolls away—
Blossoms bloom, blossoms fall.
         —Wu De (Based on an Old Zen Poem)—

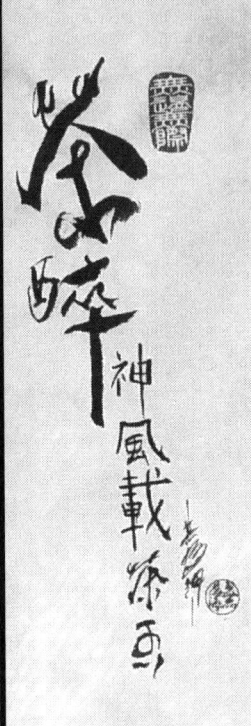

茶醉 神風載添 畫

The Eleventh Cup
Devotion

Have a cup

There was once a great calligraphy master whose entire career culminated in one brushed work, so graceful and awash with a power not his own that the artist set down his brush and retired to the mountains, never to be heard from again. The scroll read, "Devotion to Devotion." It was priceless the moment the ink touched paper, and his descendents handed it down as a family heirloom.

Several hundred years later, the brushstrokes were still radiant, though the paper had faded yellow. The master's descendents still displayed it in the alcove at special occasions. The current owner was a merchant who had lost his way, and grown miserable. A friend recommended he study tea and Zen with Master Rikyu. After a few years, the merchant was again happy and his home peaceful. He invited Rikyu over for tea, and in the tearoom displayed his family's great scroll and naught else.

When Master Rikyu arrived he bowed in obsequiousness to the old scroll, palms together as before a Zen master. And throughout the tea session, he remained as if a student—more humbled than the merchant had ever seen him before. The merchant was so impressed by his reverence, and grateful for all the master had done for him, that as they parted he handed him a box. When Rikyu got home he found that it contained the treasured scroll, which he now knew was nonpareil. It was a kingly gift.

It wasn't long before Rikyu's students learned he now owned the scroll and came over to view it. Before they did, Rikyu spent a long day and night in silent retreat before it, drinking tea alone in contemplation of the great masterpiece. He first invited his old friend, a tea master himself, named Sokyu. Sokyu was so impressed that he spilled some of his tea, though normally very calm. He exclaimed that it was the most magnificent thing he'd ever seen, and belonged more to the Heavenly realm than to this one.

The next morning a messenger arrived at Sokyu's house. Unbelievably, it was the very same scroll with a brief note from Rikyu, which said:

"Following inspiration, this travels from the inspired to those yet awaiting its touch."

A week or so later, some of Rikyu's more wealthy students arrived from distant destinations to see the fabled scroll. To their surprise, the alcove instead was adorned with a piece brushed by Rikyu's own hand: "Call on the devoted Sokyu."

While the next pot is steeping

Though the Buddha admonished us to let go of our attachment to all rites and rituals, it would be a mistake to assume that the Buddhist tradition is without devotion. Zen is a path of complete devotion. If we commit ourselves wholly to each moment in the day, there is then nothing to keep us awake at night.

Zen is a sanctification of every moment as it arises, in whatever form it manifests. The flower's grace lies, of course, in its gorgeous blossoming, but also in the poise with which it falls. And the flower doesn't submit to the Tao because it fears punishment or desires reward. True devotion is for its own sake.

Nature always acts completely. Sometimes children demonstrate this, being free of all the voices and judgments that schism an adult mind. It is difficult for us to understand how they can hate us so completely—with a rage that reddens the eyes—and then, just minutes later, be full of a love that could melt the coldest heart. This is because they are like the flower, fully committed to the moment. When they are angry there is no second-guessing or guilt. There is no reflection, just anger. And when the anger consumes itself, as it must—for no anger lasts forever—there is not a trace left. They are not then scarred by it. But the devotion of children is naïve, as is the flower's. Much more powerful is the master, who brings consciousness into her devotion.

When you have devoted yourself to the appreciation of a painting absolutely, its effect is as pure as it could be, and there is then no need to return. We only try to repeat moments that were unfulfilled. True satisfaction has always the grace to let go, for there is no need for more. When you are full, food is unappetizing.

We should view all the people and things that pass through our lives in this way, whether treasured or troubled. If you devote yourself to the enjoyment of a pleasure completely, the soul is satiated and the mind need not grasp. In that way, it takes much less to brighten your mind. Similarly, if you accept challenges utterly and pass through them devotedly, then you need not repeat the lesson a second time.

Zen is letting-go. They are synonymous. Every moment there is an acceptance and a letting-go. Zen is the grace that makes this dance beautiful. Nothing can be ripped away from an open fist. Living Zen is the art of appreciating your life so completely that you drink the tea deeply, filling all the corners of your being, then let it go just as entirely.

Ultimately, we all have to let go of ourselves. Fortunately, the great letting-go of this body is preceded by a thousand smaller ones. Absorb the calligraphy's beauty and take its meaning to heart, fully as a child would, and then pass it on to another person so that it may spread to others. Clinging and aversion are the second of the Buddha's Noble Truths, and the root of all suffering. But deep down it is our own lack of devotion that prevents us from participating in life. And we then grasp out for more, since our taste was not enough. In that state, people chase sensual pleasures, going to further and further extremes to stimulate a sense of aliveness that has really never left them. To live fully and completely does not mean without discipline. It takes great discipline to truly enjoy, for the drunkard misses too much of what he's seeing to fully appreciate it from tip to toe, the way a master does. True freedom is not when discipline is rebelliously contradicted, but rather forgotten completely and transcended.

The treasured painting is a reminder of this complete freedom, for its meaning and beauty meet between the formless and formed, as all great calligraphy does. And you cannot say that Rikyu is incapable of appreciating the work, as his reverence clearly shows otherwise. Some commentators have suggested that he gave the painting away because it distracted from the tea, being too beautiful—causing even adept hands like Sokyu's to fumble. That is true—let those looking for a show call on Sokyu—but this is just the surface. It is also important to understand why Rikyu could pass the painting on: because he had enjoyed it so fully.

Zen tea is prepared and drunk with such complete devotion, and not a drop then remains at the end of the session. Sometimes *Chajin* share tea at a shop or friend's home, and if it is good, immediately respond with a desire to possess it. They didn't enjoy it enough to leave it there. They didn't really empty the cup; some dregs remain at the bottom. Practice emptying your cup. In that way, there is room for other teas. If you drink with all of yourself, the tea is the same Tao which moves the world—its Qi then becomes you, and you no longer need a cup or leaves to feel it. Rikyu often said that the *Chajin*—tea person—should "imagine a life without tea, and if it is any different from your life now, you have yet to truly understand tea." Learn to appreciate how beautiful the empty cup is—just as wonderful as the full one!

A tea master I know once decided to break up a very, very expensive cake of vintage Puerh tea. It just so happened that a visitor arrived in the shop just as he was doing this. The man was in awe. He almost dropped his jaw on the floor. He wondered aloud if we knew how much money the tea was worth, and how we could possibly break it up and drink it. "As for the *how*, that's easy as you can see," smiled the master, as he tore off a chunk, "and if you want to know *why*, have a seat." A couple hours and many, many cups later the session ended. "I understand," was all the man said as he left.

I am not the one that loves; it's love that seizes me.
—Leonard Cohen—

The Twelfth Cup

A Returning to Softness

Have a cup

The noble Lin received some very high-quality spring tribute tea from an associate in the palace. He hoped to share it with Master Lu Yu, and so quickly dispatched an invitation to the mountain where he dwelt. The old master replied from his hermitage that it was his virtue to never, ever refuse an invitation to have tea.

Having studied the old master's books, the noble Lin knew that the water gathered just after the Tiger Falls at a relatively still spot surrounded by current was ideal for such green tea. However, he quickly became busy with preparations for the master's visit and postponed the trip until the very day of Lu Yu's arrival.

He woke up especially early that day, sincerely wishing to draw the water with his own hands. Such was an honor, and not for the servants. They found the spot Lu Yu had written of, and amazingly it was a calm oasis within a rush of eddies, as if the river itself took a rest there. The noble Lin filled a stone jar to take back with them. Unfortunately, as they neared the shore, the boatman came aground on a stone and the boat was rocked violently, spilling a third of the precious water—and there wasn't time to return to the source. "Effort is most of it," realized the noble Lin, so he topped the jar off with water from the shore, thinking no one would ever be the wiser.

The master arrived, and though they had never met before, they greeted one another like old friends—as tea lovers then and now are the world over wont to do. When the tea was prepared, its fresh aroma filled the room and everyone smiled in satisfaction. Lu Yu was very pleased, and reverently bowed to the noble Lin, thanking him for the opportunity to share such wonderful tea in such a nice setting. He closed his eyes to converse with the tea, but his host wished to have other conversations: "I gathered this water myself from the 'Calm Eye,' just past the Tiger Falls," he said obsequiously. A single white eyebrow raised in askance, and the lid beneath fluttered open. The old master clucked his tongue, "Hmmmm… really?" He paused and cocked his ear up, as though listening to a distant sound. "I think you should have left well enough alone. Though this tea has such water in it, it was diluted with inferior water from elsewhere, was it not? I would guess you weren't mindful and spilled some along the way."

The noble Lin bowed down in awe and apologized profusely. Master Lu Yu stayed him with his hand, "the words were more detrimental to the tea than the water. Enjoy it as it is, and I promise I will too." His admonishment and smile were so heartfelt that the noble Lin did indeed relax and enjoy the rest of the afternoon in silence. His embarrassment vanished, and the two parted life-long friends.

While the next pot is steeping

The Zen circle, or "Enshu", is a loop from the gross to the subtle, and back again to the gross—like the orbiting monks who circumambulate the center of the meditation hall to allow a similar, though internal, circulation to return to their legs. We must learn to quiet the outside and return to the softness that is the chewy center of our beings. The Zen painter-monk Sengai once drew an *Enshu* and wrote calligraphy next to it that said, "Eat this and have some tea!"

As we shift focus from doing to just *being*, the world naturally turns inward. It requires no effort on our part; it's as natural as the flow of water downhill. When distractions are shut off, and outer quietude cultivated, stillness just happens. Even the most silted, muddy water clarifies itself when it is tranquil—all the more the vast depths of the lake, ever unruffled by the Worldly breezes that ripple its surface.

For stillness to flourish, however, our posture is important: we must be upright, firmly rooted in the earth with our head held high in the sky. Our adroitness is not tense, because there is a grace in this poise, like a dancer balanced, twirling on her toes. The best meditation (*Zazen*) comes from this posture, and some masters have taught that such a posture is completion, without remainder. In an upright posture, the mind naturally and without effort begins to settle into quietude; and as it quiets down our true nature—which was there all along—shines forth from out of the space we've just made. With a bit of inner emptiness, the world and

Truth come rushing into our open hearts. The best tea is also prepared in such a posture, unaffected though upright Within the Chinese character for "Tao" is the radical for the "upright man", because the ancients knew how important our spines were, likening the spiritual journey to a vertical dimension which is perpendicular to the horizontally mundane flow of time from past to future.

But Zen can never be forced. There is no ultimate subtlety you can sell in a book or carry around in your pocket. The secret of the universe isn't even knowable. You are living it. In being alive, the world is experiencing itself through you; and when you set aside the distinction between your mind and the world, and let outer quietude harmonize with inner stillness, the Buddha then meditates, not you.

Most of our day is devoted to doing, always focused on the outward—actively pursuing this or that. But then the rhythms of nature strum in discord to our lives, and the sound is clashing and odious. This noise disrupts the peace of individuals and whole societies. Nature always balances times of stillness with activity—day and night, winter and summer, foraging and hibernation. For most people, however, the noise of our daily activities leaves us restless at night as well.

Through the last few centuries, we have developed amazing technology, harnessing the power of the human intellect: we've connected the globe through computers, breached the heavens with aviation and space travel, and even extended the normal life-span through medical advancements. Nevertheless, in order to focus exclusively on the rational part of ourselves, we have for the most part abandoned another, older intelligence: a feeling of being connected to the world, which you could call "instinct" or "intuition". Being a part of Nature came naturally to our ancestors, as it does to plants and animals. They didn't just study the stars or seasons, they felt a part of them—in harmony with the dance. The distinction between the mind and the world wasn't as gross, in other words. Lost in our minds, and an endless stream of dialogue about our doings, comings and goings—work, entertainment and personal drama—our connection to Nature has all but fallen to the wayside.

And yet, it would be further delusion to glorify the lives of our ancestors (and Zen is always about Reality). Such a life had its hardships. We cannot go back, and who would want to discard many of the useful and wonderful innovations we've created and discovered. Our future is forward. But we mustn't stop learning from the ancients, though we don't ape them. We must continue to be able to harness the intellect, while at the same time not be ruled by it. To govern the mind and its power, as a secondary instrument of our beings—which are in accord with Nature and the Tao, and always were—is the divine life, as an individual and as a species.

One of the most resonant of our dissonant chords, in this modern life, is just this very hyperactivity. We need to remember, as does Nature, that there is a time for rest and a time for vigor, a time for growth and another for decay. To align ourselves with the coming together of energy works much better than trying to force Nature to behave in the way we want it to, just as it is important to appreciate the periods of dissolution and face them with openness, honesty and acceptance, rather than trying to hide death and disease, or regard them as unmentionables. The current carries us whether we want it to our not, and fighting it only makes the journey seem troubled and pointless. But there is a skill to navigating the river, using its currents—deft placement of an oar here or there to steer the boat. That is where Zen comes in: Zen is life's paddle, you could say.

The Buddha separated his 'Eight Fold Path' into "skillful", "whole-some" or "balanced" means—depending on how you translate the Pali word "samma". Zen is all about coursing this life more skillfully and grace-fully, not resounding lightning powers of Enlightenment (with a capital E). It is skillful to seek emptier, quieter spaces now and again. Of course, a much more powerful Zen is one in which we can stay connected to empty space while in the midst of activity, but even thus we must return to the well of outer space and quietude now and again to drink and replenish our soul. Zen is but the *upaya* to traverse this life.

As soon as the body is postured, the mind settles. The fact that this is a necessary part of human development—like air, food or water—should be obvious, since the movement inwards occurs naturally as soon as distractions are cut off and the body settled. Our ancestors achieved this by living and eating simply. After a hard day's work, they slept soundly and naturally. There is an old Chinese tale of a farmer who shooed the mechanical pump salesman away, arguing that he would corrupt his grand-son's mind, which was still young and impressionable. "I know what he doesn't," exclaimed the old farmer, clarifying: "If I mechanize everything,

I will have nothing to be; and finding myself useless, how will I sleep at night?"

Our hearts beat themselves, and trillions of processes all happen to us and within us every day. If we had to control even a fraction of the functions that are balanced perfectly by Nature within our bodies, we'd have time for nothing else in a day. The capacity for clarity and peace is already within you, as is the ability to perceive clearly. As soon as you leave the city behind, you realize the birdsong and river arpeggio were always playing. It was you who needed tuning.

As you allow stillness to permeate your life, you more and more recognize the movement towards softness, and you grow more and more sensitive. The breath naturally becomes softer and softer as the mind quiets—it does this, not you. It is a natural movement of Nature, requiring no human intervention. You just observe—be an open space, awareness—ready for whatever arises, like the empty cup. Your mind may wander. Let it. There is nothing to do… just *be* and let whatever happens occur on its own.

Tea can be a great aid in cultivating outer quietude and inner stillness—Zen and tea are, after all, one flavor. It's hard to talk with a mouth full of tea. Besides, the tea wants you to be quiet. It invites you inward. At first you notice only gross flavors, but over time your tea drinking more and more becomes a time of quiet rest, introspection and stillness. This happens naturally. Then, you begin noticing more and more flavors, as if the tea were rewarding you for your newfound peace. You begin to notice things beyond the flavor and aroma. There are sensations: the way the tea touches the mouth and throat, and returns on the breath. Over time, these also become softer and softer, clearer and clearer as you become more sensitive. This only happens when there is outer quietude, which leads to inner stillness; and it isn't long before you realize that your own state of mind is the most important ingredient in the tea—it's not which tea or teaware, but how it's prepared. Eventually, you begin to experience the movement of what Chinese call "Qi". This is the living energy within our bodies. Whether you move your foot or not you know it's there, even with your eyes closed, because you can feel it from the inside. You are feeling the electricity traveling through nerves to your brain, atomic movement and energy, Qi, or whatever else you wish to call it. Fine tea catalyzes this energy, causing it to move, and if you are quiet—without and within—you will begin to feel it.

The Chinese call the tea ceremony "gong fu tea". This "gong fu", means with skill and mastery. It refers to the art of living through all things, completely in tune with the Tao of that thing—the Way its tendency moves towards—the Way it "wants" to be completed, in other words. And there are many legends of simple people defeating master martial artists with tea: intent on battle, they were pacified and the tea brewer was therefore victorious.

You might think Lu Yu's sensitivity is just a fable, too fantastical to be true, but as you begin to allow yourself to spend as much time being as doing—and let life turn inward—you'll realize it isn't that far-fetched at all. The connection is already there. Your mind is not separate from this world, but arose out of it. Every particle of every atom in your body was once in a star. The feeling of connection is inborn, founded upon a real, undivided, non-dual world. Similarly, there is no distinction between life and tea. You might think that someone so caught up in holding tea sessions might like a day or two vacation away from it now and then, only to find that the *Chajin* takes his teaware to the mountain with him—committed, each day then is itself the Way of Tea.

Tea in every way epitomizes the traditional Chinese attitudes to Nature, the seasons and changes. There is a time for rest and sensitivity to it, ignored at the peril of your health. Though Lu Yu often discusses tea's virtues in terms of such health, praising it for the alertness it offers, etc., it was this subtlety, sensitivity and stillness that were at the heart of his devotion to tea. Lao Tzu also said that the Tao was a returning to softness. Through skill, loving attention to detail and spirit tea opens us up—like so many twirling dervish-leaves—open to Nature's melodies as they play around, through and within us so that we once again live in concordance, indistinct from the world and its Way.

The doorway to Zen is always unlocked. The gateway is the body and mind you now experience, not some other. Find the time to just have some tea. All these words are good if they help direct you to that place. Otherwise, as Lu Yu suggested in the story, the words just ruin the tea—more than any bad water ever could.

Become mind's master, not mind-mastered.
                              —Murata Juko—

The Thirteenth Cup
Gunpowder Tea

Have a cup

There was once an old master that lived in the remote mountains. He never taught a single sermon, and yet the isolation and lack of formal Zen didn't stop him from gathering some students, lured there by the serenity that misted around his monastery and his eyes. Instead of teaching, he would just prepare tea, asking only that anyone who wished to learn with him keep the moral precepts and drink tea in quiet. Every gesture of his hand spoke in hushed whispers of a peace just up the next trail, now briefly glimpsed for the first time as the mists and clouds are momentarily parted by a breeze. There was no ceremony, though. He didn't whisk tea like the monks in the lowlands. His way was much simpler: He taught the monks to tend the old tea trees near the monastery, only taking a small amount for each day. They would process it early in the morning before dawn and leave it to rest as they went about farming and other daily chores. In the early evening, he would then scatter these leaves in a bowl and cover them with steaming spring water he had gathered himself from the nearby stream. This was his discourse. This was his Zen.

No words could ever describe the peace such a draught inspired, as if it were indeed the Morning Dew that granted wayward hermits immortality. It was hard to pass on his teaching, or understand it even, though the effect was there—that's what made it Zen!

Over time, the old master also attracted some lay disciples as well, who made the long trek to his hermitage once or twice a year to spend a month basking in the peaceful surroundings. When they returned to the World of Dust their friends and loved ones would notice the change the trip had brought about in them.

A noble disciple of the master was holding a tea gathering of other wealthy connoisseurs, and amongst the many topics they discussed—mostly about nice teaware, art and fine tea—the master's disciple spoke up, saying that the greatest tea he'd ever had was so simple. He tried to somehow put the master's silent teaching into words, telling the others that the quality of the tea and teaware didn't matter half as much as the hand that prepared it. But his words fell short, and the others couldn't help but smile politely, not really understanding what he was getting at. "I admit; it is really difficult to explain... He is so at peace that you, yourself cannot help but be tranquil when you're around him... and this somehow—in some strange way—reaches out from his tea... Alas!" he sighed, not knowing what else to say.

A rich cloth merchant scoffed, saying: "Anyone can be at peace in the mountains, where there is no sound or distraction and the air and water are so clean and pure. Of course such tea will be good, grown so high and brewed with such water. The fact that you felt peaceful drinking it was just the good tea and water, as well as the nice surroundings. It had little to do with the one making the tea." The noble didn't know how to respond. Another of the merchants saw an opportunity for some amusement, as well as a wager and a plan was hatched. The master's student knew in his heart it was wrong, but the others had put his honor at stake. He, therefore, reluctantly agreed.

The old master was invited to come to drink tea. He agreed, and three students accompanied him down the mountains to the city. As they were walking through the garden towards the tearoom, it had been arranged for several of the merchants' guards to fire guns at the master and his students from some hidden bushes—without loading shot into the muskets, of course, only powder.

And so, as the master and his three students got to the middle of the garden, a barrage of gunfire sounded—all aimed in their direction. The three students scattered—falling to the ground, rolling around and, in one case, even running from the garden altogether. To the astonishment of the noble and merchants, who watched from the threshold of the tearoom where they stood as hosts, the old master didn't even lose a single stride. His peaceful bearing deflected the noise as would the highest castle wall, and there was not even a twitch in his face. His downcast eyes, serene gait and poise passed through the violence as casually as if it hadn't happened, and he were just out for a stroll amongst the monastery gardens. Ignoring even his students' antics, he made his way to the tearoom porch and greeted his hosts, removed his shoes and entered without a word about the noise.

While the next pot is steeping

We start by finding a quiet space to sit in *Zazen* or drink tea, and our thoughts settle and clarify. We all need such time. Long ago, even merchants, so busy with work, life and drama, still had gardens and tearooms that they occasionally retreated to in order to be like hermits—if only for a few hours. But such outer silence and peace are easily shattered, especially nowadays. Even a mountain hermitage might be disturbed by an airplane passing overhead; and if your peace and quiet is only in this solitude, how fragile it is, indeed. Also, even in the mountains, all the vicissitudes of human suffering follow you, and haunt your mind. Though it is important to seek some quiet space to just be, inner stillness is where the really good tea is prepared. Make sure you don't miss the inner session!

We practice making our lives into a space that has enough cleanliness, purity and tranquility to promote inner stillness. That is the outer garb of Buddhism and Zen. The Buddha himself often referred to all the meditations, precepts and guidelines as "tools" or a "raft" to cross the river of human suffering. This was just a metaphor, expressing the greater importance of the wordless, inexpressible wisdom you already are—the flower he offered Kashyapa.

Zen was the first monastic tradition to be self-sustaining. The fourth and fifth patriarchs established large monasteries based on agriculture, and promoted the famous Zen ideal: "No work, no food." The monks of India, on the other hand, survived by begging, devoting their lives to meditation. In Zen, practice was not to be distinguished from life, and isolated to a particular place or posture. Walking, gardening, cleaning and farming are all opportunities to meditate. More tea and less talk, study and meditation, in other words.

All the movement of this universe is contained within a great stillness. Without space, the stars would collapse and all would be consumed in light. All the matter in existence is but a decimal point of endless space. And scientists are now coming to realize what the Buddha taught millennia ago: that within each and every atom, there is mostly space as well. Even the matter, itself contained in space, is in essence just more space. Emptiness is form, and form emptiness.

It is the space within the teapot that makes it useful, not the clay. And we are like teapots: filled with space we are capable of form. The best teapots, though, influence whatever you put in them—even mediocre tea and water is transformed and made better for having passed through such a space. The teapot gives up its emptiness for the sake of the leaf. The master also adds such golden tinges to the liquor of life by identifying as much with the space within her as she does with the form. Like the famous Zen master, she can say, "Is that so?", to whatever passes through her experience, recognizing that it is transient and let it unfold as it would, just so. He was prominent until a teenage girl accused him of molesting her and causing her pregnancy. "Is that so?", was all he said—and again when they brought him the baby to care for. He raised the child for some time, and even grew quite fond of it. But he again said only, "Is that so?", when the girl, years later, confessed that the father was actually the fish-monger's son, and the family came to apologize and take the child back home with them. Is that so?

It may seem like this attitude is apathetic, but if you really look a bit closer, you'll see that so many of life's challenges could skillfully be avoided or faced with a bit of space to let them be. In a cluttered World, space is the most valuable commodity: a painting is more beautiful alone in empty space, just as people transform amazingly when given the space to do so. Even when it comes time to act, the master will do so much more skillfully having first allowed the situation the space to breathe. She will then see the inclination of the Tao, and know where her hand will have the greatest effect.

Often times we feel as if we don't have enough space to contain a situation, and react against it. We try to push it away, fight it or deny its existence altogether. But emptiness has no real boundaries. It cannot even be defined, though we can point at it. Actually, there is within you enough space to contain worlds. This universe has room for whatever arises, cosmically or in the corner of the Earth you occupy.

When you identify as much with the empty stillness within you as you do with the form you realize that there is nothing added or taken away from this world—realize it at the fundamental, living level, not as an intellectual idea. You must live this connection, not speak it. You pour it and drink it in your tea, like the master. It is real, physical and concrete. It is impossible to disturb the peace of space, for it can contain any phenomena in the universe—even cataclysmic stellar explosions! Death itself is just another such change, and the master accepts that too, just as the Earth and space do.

Nothing can threaten you when you are grounded in inner stillness, for you don't have anything that can be taken away. You are not diminished by your own death even, for the loss of the body does not hinder the space—the transformation of form is contained within the emptiness, in other words.

The master in this cup-story acts within the World as anyone else—he walks and talks, sheds hair and loses teeth—but inwardly, he is still. His quiet is not the quiet of the mountain, peaceful for all to see, but the quiet of empty space. Even if the world erupted apocalyptically, space wouldn't bat an eye. In harmony with the universe, the Earth also does not distinguish between gunfire and music. They are both just sound—waves passing through air. Though his mind recognizes the gunfire as such, and probably also realizes the game his student is playing, the master does not discriminate. There is room in his being for a bit of loud noise.

This kind of acceptance is an ideal, one we all strive for. The more you identify with the quiet on the outside, the more your inner stillness will respond. Try reminding yourself that you are big enough to contain whatever arises in your life, and that the ups and downs are all a part of one mountain chain. A tea lover named Hechikan once spent a lot of time criticizing Rikyu. He then invited him to tea one day. Rikyu knew some mischief was at hand, but like Master Lu Yu before him he practiced the virtue of never declining an invitation to tea, even from a so-called "enemy". When he got there he saw the ruse: a muddy puddle covered with leaves right along the path to the tearoom, and there at the door were several lords and famous nobles watching him approach. With a child's grace, Rikyu knowingly walked into the puddle, affecting some drama for Hechikan's sake. His host then took him to the bathhouse in feigned obsequiousness, apologizing profusely, which meant Rikyu would quite-embarrassingly miss the tea gathering. He pretended to be humiliated, allowing Hechikan his fun, and meanwhile enjoyed his bath, napping in the warm water.

Start simply, that is what the master in this cup-story is teaching: Pacify your tea. Make sure you pour the water gracefully and silently. Be that pouring, rather than separate from it as the one who does it. When you are it, the stillness is there. Tea is a metaphor for life, and quite poignantly it is also life itself. It's not that the Zen masters wanted us to cultivate still-ness and awareness, or the equanimity demonstrated in this cup-story, only while drinking tea. That would be moving the certain place/certain posture from the meditation hall to the tearoom—escaping one trap only to be mired in the muck of another. The old hermit in this story is not a "Zen Buddhist"; he just makes tea. And yet, is he not more Zen than the temple priest? But if you then call him a "Teaist", he'll put his pot and kettle aside and serve you some cabbage soup.

Zen is a return to the purity of living wisdom in all that we do. Tea is just another way of pointing this out, sometimes better because it is beyond words. A tea ceremony is ideal for this, resting as it does on the border between action and silent meditation—stillness within movement. Remember: "No work, no food." And the real crop of the Zen monastery isn't the cabbage or tea, but stillness.

A cup ever full,
Brimming with presence.
A cup ever empty,
Silent, awaiting the next.
                    —Wu De—

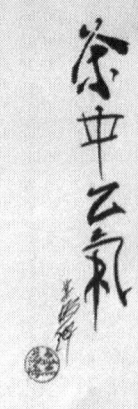

The Fourteenth Cup

A Butterfly's Dream of Manhood

Have a cup

One bright dawn in a secluded monastery, the old master Gui Shan was just beginning to stir. His senior disciple Yang Shan entered the room and prostrated before his teacher. The old master groaned and rolled over to face the wall as if he wasn't done sleeping and the student had disturbed him. But Yang Shan was wise to his teacher's constant antics: "I am your student and attendant, master. There is no need to behave so formally," he jibbed. Gui Shan rolled over and sat up, rubbing his eyes with his fists.

"Come and hear about my dream, son."

Yang Shan sat down to listen, though the old man didn't say a word about his dream. As soon as Yang Shan was settled, the master instead commanded him, "Now that you've heard about my dream, interpret it for me!" Yang Shan got up and brought the pan of warm water and towel from the stoop, which he had come to bring his master in the first place. Gui Shan washed and dried his face and hands, beaming at his student with the brightest of smiles.

At that moment, another of his senior disciples, Xiang Yun, was passing by the master's open door. "Ah, young Xiang Yun," began the master, "It's turning out to be a wonderful morning. Yang Shan and I were just having a mystical, spiritual union. That is no small thing!"

"I couldn't help but overhear, master."

"Then perhaps you also could help me interpret my dream," replied the master.

Xiang Yun smiled in acquiescence. He sat before the master and brought out the bowl from his bag. He put some tea leaves in it and covered it with steaming water from the kettle that was boiling in the anteroom. He bowed and passed it to his master, in answer to his dream. The master inhaled the steam deeply, took a sip and exclaimed: "Truly, my students have surpassed me!"

While the next pot is steeping

The Buddha taught that life should be viewed as if it were a dream, illusionary and fleeting. He didn't argue a philosophy in saying so, because he did not comment on the way things *are*, just that it was useful *upaya* to look at them in this way—*as if* they were a dream, which doesn't mean they necessarily are. Set aside arguments and philosophies for a moment of clarity: What happens when you see the world this way? Not so much to think about how fleeting life is, or to philosophize on its oneiric qualities, but actually *see* life in this way with your eyes, touch it with your hands, etc. What does a dream feel like and how does it differ from your so-called "waking" moments?

In ancient tales, the word "doom" was also used to refer to one's fate—future, in other words. And this is what the Buddha meant. We are all, in the end, doomed: glorious king and suffering leper alike. If you ever doubt how much you have in common with your fellow man, look to your doom; if you ever think you've found lasting peace through some relationship, to someone or something, look to your doom; and if you ever feel challenged by something you think is permanent and insurmountable, look to your doom. Do you want to live a good life (and who doesn't?): then find your doom! If you asked a shaman—from the time when America was young and green—what she wanted from life, "a good death" would be the answer, for only a good life can end well. "Ho Hota Hey!" The tribe would chorus behind her answer: "Today is a good day to die!"

Is that enough of a pin prick? Can you cast off the Sandman's dust?

Seeing through illusion is skillful means—*upaya*. The ancients believed that once you knew the demon's name, exorcism was easy. The dark ignorance flees from the light of awareness—when we become conscious of the mind it no longer holds sway, in other words. Seeing, as opposed to understanding, lets us know what is primary and what is secondary—what is important and what isn't. Zen isn't about philosophizing your way out of Reality towards salvation in some paradisiacal realm. In fact, if Zen had to be categorized as some kind of ism, rather than Buddhism, I would say that true Zen is Realism: *seeing the Truth as it is.*

This tradition of Shaking off the Dust and shedding the mind was passed on from India to China; it was the flower held up on Vulture Peak, the sixth patriarch Hui Neng's shaking of the sieve, and also the Japanese master Dogen's "falling away of body and mind". See what happens when you too look at this world as mind-made. See that when the mind arises, the whole universe appears.

Hui Neng once came upon two monks arguing over a pendant that was fluttering in a morning breeze. One said it was the flag that moved, while the other argued that the flag didn't move at all—only the wind. When they asked the master for his opinion, he admonished them both, saying: "Neither the wind nor the flag moves, only the mind!" What, then, happens when the mind is gone?

This doesn't mean Zen is pessimistic and depressed. On the contrary, passing through this life as though it were a dream affords one a kind of playful wonder, without any of the needless attachment. There are situations we can neither change nor escape, some of which are indeed ugly to behold, but our relationship to life as it passes by can be *upaya*. In accepting change gracefully, you can enjoy the times of summer without feeling depressed when the weather grows cold. And in the barren snow, when all is cold and lifeless, there is also a beauty—an aesthetic of pain and great insight in suffering. The very word "buddha" means "awakened one". And awakening from the dream usually happens with a bit of tossing and turning. Who wants to wake up from a good dream? Those that have passed through some suffering often have a greater insight into life, in other words. Having faced their doom, they now see what is primary and what is secondary.

There is a story of a samurai who visited a famous Zen master. When he looked down into his bowl of tea he saw a snake. He looked in askance at the master, whose calm demeanor betrayed nothing. The proud warrior swallowed his pride and then the snake with a grimace. His stomach ached in pain. Once again he sternly confronted the master with furrowed brow and piercing eyes—shaking with a warrior's caged pride and rage. The master glanced up to the ceiling and the samurai followed his gaze to the vivid image of a snake painted there, reflective in the dim light.

In Zen, the dream itself is the foundation of our practice. You have to be careful talking of this, though. It is easy to get confused and "build a nest in the secondary", as they say. It is not enough to simply proclaim that enlightenment and the World are one in the same (*Nibbana = Samsara*) sigh "ho-hum" and then do any old thing you please. Nor is this way of looking at life—as but the reflection of swans in a still lake—meant to inspire a breed of nihilism, though it does involve a glimpse or two into the Void. Not everything needs to have an expressible purpose; some things can be done for their own sake. Perhaps life is one such thing?

Zen does focus on the ordinary life itself, rather than transcendent states of no-mind, but you cannot say that it is simply any way of life, either. There is some inexpressible difference between Zen tea and the tea they serve in the boisterous teahouse, though this difference weighs less than a speck of dust. Perhaps it is the experience of passing through meditation, and no-mind, and then returning to the ordinary—perhaps not. What do you think?

Gui Shan and his students understand that chopping wood and making a fire are themselves great teachings of the emptiness in form, and form in emptiness. The universe itself is *being* its own lesson. And yet, humans the world over are working and living, manifesting anger and violence, greed and destruction. There is something, after all, in the realization itself—a change in the way you chop wood and make a fire when it is Zen. But it isn't logical, and there's no way to wrap your mind around it. That's where the tea comes in.

In Zen this body and this mind are everything. This cup of tea is life's interpretation of itself. There is a very real mystical communion in this act: sun and moonshine, mountain air and water all absorbed by a leaf and used to grow, which you then steep in hot water and consume—dissolving in your body and becoming the elements of your own living form. The universe meets itself in the ordinary moment in a billion ways, some we can see and some we cannot. There's no need to search for magic in other worlds when this one will do just fine.

The simpler your life is, the easier Zen practice begins. Clutter is detrimental to our health, of mind and body. Simplify everything. This is easy to do when you look to your doom. Everything is impermanent, and there is no future where or when to rest or be complete. There is no need to be preoccupied with preparations towards a future life when you are already alive now, and already complete. You cannot possibly be any more alive than you are. Seeing the world in this way is skillful means (*upaya*), since it gets the mind out of the way. As soon as we get out of the way of ourselves, the world moves through us; and we then begin recognizing currents we hadn't realized before. Navigation becomes much easier. Only when the world is viewed through a human mind is there a problem to be fixed. No mind, no problem.

"That's it?", you ask. "Just drink tea? Could it be thus? Shouldn't it be hidden in Himalayan monasteries or on saffroned scrolls?" But the world, in all its myriad forms, is now manifesting in this shape. Pick up your bowl. The warmth is real. It awakens. If you drink deeply, the whole world is drunk up. And there's no dust in the empty bowl, wet and shiny… just a few tea dregs.

To rest in the arms of perfection is the desire of any man intent upon creating excellence; and is not nothingness a form of perfection?

—Thomas Mann—

The Fifteenth Cup
Lost — Trained — Found

Have a cup 🍵

From a very early age the noble Lin's third son Chung Chi was inclined towards the religious life, and it was therefore no surprise when he came of age and asked his father for permission to leave the household, casting off the Red Dust of the World. His father assented and blessed him for the last time.

Chung Chi spent ten years living in a monastery at the foot of the mountains. He was a devoted monk and walked with reverence. He was humble before his master, the abbot, though often distant. His heart lay deeper into the forest, higher in the mountains. The comings and goings of lay people and all the rituals, as well as work, distracted him. He felt his answers were in the heavier waters at the bottom of the lake.

Like any master should, the old abbot saw this sorrow in Chung Chi's eyes. One day, as they were drinking tea, the master told him: "Near here, deep in the mountains, past the oldest tree and Dragon Falls, there is a monk like you. He was once my dharma brother. We shared the same master—the previous abbot. When our master passed away, we agreed that I would stay here and run the monastery and he would retreat to the mountains to find enlightenment. He promised that if he found the Shadowy Portal he would leave me a sign, to comfort me in my old age. One morning, I found this at my door…" He handed Chung Chi a shiny, black stone. It seemed otherworldly, humming with power. It was translucent and glassy, and he could see himself reflected wavy and distorted in its depths. "Take it," continued the old monk, "and go find him. He knows all about that which you seek."

Chung Chi thanked his master and headed off into the mountains. He searched for days all around the Dragon Falls, but found nothing. After two weeks he gave up and returned to the monastery. He wasn't crestfallen, though. He had permission to wander, which put his heart at ease. Once every fortnight, he would leave before dawn and spend a few days roaming the mountains—an occasional, reassuring touch to the stone in his pocket, encouraging him to hope. Just knowing that enlightenment was possible for him was solace enough.

After a year or so, Chung Chi finally stumbled upon a small clearing, and there beneath some very old tea trees was a small hut. He waited there a few days, but no one came. Having a destination made the walk into the mountains all the more enjoyable, as did the warm hut to sleep in. The master was never there, but Chung Chi began to care less and less as time passed. He started finding great joy in the walk—the mountain air, clean water and quiet hut. He was in no hurry. He had the stone and knew where the hut was.

Over the years, Chung Chi's trips to the mountain hut changed him. Even his duties at the monastery weren't so bad. He began to accept them, sometimes even enjoying the rituals and chanting. The mountain seclusion and communal life in the monastery began to be stitched into the robes of a single life, the distinction fading away over time.

Around that time, Chung Chi returned to the hut one day and to his great surprise found that the fire was still burning, the coals still alight under a thin layer of ash. And there on the table was a tea bowl and some leaves from the nearby trees. He was radiant, thinking the hermit had surely left these for him—which meant he knew he was there. He drank the tea and sat enjoying the quiet of the hut. This continued, and each time Chung Chi arrived the tea, bowl, fire and water would be waiting for him.

A few more years passed and Chung Chi forgot all about the master and his quest. He still went to the hut, but it was for the tea, fresh air and quietude. He'd meditate and drink tea there for a few days and return to the monastery when his food ran out. One autumn afternoon Chung Chi was sitting in the hut. He had just finished his tea and was meditating contentedly, noticing how marvelously the trees changed colors. He was very surprised to hear some footsteps approaching. A shadow filled the doorway. When the figure stepped in out of the light, Chung Chi was amazed to see the abbot, his own master, standing there. Chung Chi understood everything. He prostrated himself. Then, rising up, he opened the old man's hand and placed the worn stone in his palm. He didn't need it anymore.

While the next pot is steeping

In all the vast volumes of *sutras* the Buddha taught over 47 years the word "Nibbana" is barely mentioned at all. He never spoke of enlightenment, and dismissed inquiries when it did come up—usually by witty scholars or monks trying to intellectualize. Instead, he taught about this life: our own winding way across this earth. You can't practice what is taught anyway, and there is no need to discuss the things that should be lived.

When you get rid of ideas of enlightenment and delusion a lot of mind-made complications also dissolve. The idea that Truth is only living in remote mountains is one such distinction. The Tao is the movement of this universe, in all places and even through humanity and all its creations. It is difficult sometimes to recognize that the side of human existence we label "negative" is also a part of this vast and perfect universe. We want to envision imaginary worlds where such things as human greed and violence don't exist, but those worlds aren't *real*. We live in this one; and in this world human nature is thus—as it is. "Ya ta bhu ta" were words the Buddha did repeat often—unlike "enlightenment"—and they mean precisely that: "as it is, not as you would like it to be." Only when the sacred and profane have unified can you see what the Buddha meant by "suchness" and why he called himself "Tathagata"—"the one who has walked thus."

In ancient China, before the dawn of civilization, sages were seeking to communicate with the universe by retreating to the mountains where they could look deeper into themselves. With great insight, they chose to call the great movement of this cosmos "Tao", which means the "way" or "path". It is of course impossible to capture the universe and condense its meaning into a word, but in reference to that movement why not choose a word like this, which already corresponds with the road we all travel—making the journey of our life itself a reference point towards ultimate Truth.

When you are searching for something and working towards something, you lose sight of the path, focusing instead on some imaginary goal. And the path is the Path, which means that your own silly game is stopping you from seeing that which you yourself are looking for. Instead, seek out the universal in the particular: find the Tao of Cha, and you'll have found the Tao.

When you are bent towards the goal of a new and better you, the focus is still on the ego—albeit a bright, shiny and golden ego. Only when the monk in this cup-story stopped looking and started enjoying the mountain paths for their own sake did the master start leaving him some warm tea to refresh the end of his journey. And only when the journey and goal had both been forgotten, merging into non-duality, did the master himself appear to verify his student's awakening—though he had actually been there all along. Everything becomes alright when we stop seeking—the answers just fall into our laps.

In the annals of Zen, masters often use the metaphor of "strolling through the mountains" to refer to an existential freedom from logic and discriminative thought patterns, wandering free of all attachments, as the monk began to do in this cup-story. Thus in the famous *koan*, the student asks the great master Chang Sha exactly where he'd gone on his "stroll". "First, I followed the aroma of fragrant grasses, then I returned trailing scattered blossoms." He rejoins.

The true master works from a distance, until the student is ready to recognize how ordinary a master is. Then the game of master and student is seen for what it is: more drama. In drinking the tea and walking to and from the hut, the monk found the insight himself. This cannot be taught, because it's already here. You just need to discover that you are what you seek, and then all seeking ceases. Then you can have a cup of tea.

My master can teach of Zen and meditation, or even answer philosophical questions; but all that is too often confused with ego stuff: isms and schisms, arguments about points of logic, traditions, opinions and beliefs. He can fulfill that role, but it isn't the one he shines in. If you instead ask him with earnestness how to clean a teapot, his eyes light up and everyone around becomes transfixed in Presence—here and now focused on this teapot and its cleaning. Could there be a better discourse on Zen?

The greatest truths aren't just in the forest or mountains. Even if you move to the mountains, won't you bring your mind? Would you be seeking states you thought were higher or better? And would your mind think you had achieved something through your renunciation?

Maybe it's better to let go of enlightenments and delusions and just see how alive you are. Isn't it marvelous that the universe evolved from stars to minerals, minerals to life—and then after eons transformed into these very eyes and mouth?

If it helps, rub the Zen stone—knowing that the masters and buddhas of before have left us *sutras* to show that enlightened living is possible. But try to drink as much tea as you can, living here in your only life. Then maybe one day you will also find you can return the stone, sure that there is always another empty pot waiting to be filled with leaf.

Leaves and water
Crafted by the heart,
Not the hand.
Prepare tea without preparing,
In the stillness at the center of Being.
                                   —Wu De—

The Sixteenth Cup
The Best Tea Session

Have a cup

There were three samurai that met regularly for tea. All of them had studied for decades, and they considered themselves spiritual brothers since they were all students of the same Zen master.

One fine day they met for tea, sitting in silence by a creek, listening to it rattle on over flattened stones like distant *sutras* chanted by a chorus of monastics. After some time, they decided to have a walk, the Qi from the seven bowls of tea they'd enjoyed pleasantly carrying them onward. They talked openly and freely, without any of the semblance they ordinarily adhered to in society. Part of why they gathered, in fact, was to abandon their roles and responsibilities for a time. Somehow the conversation turned to the best tea sessions they had ever had.

The first samurai captivated them with a story of a pilgrimage he'd taken years ago with their Zen master. On their way to a distant temple, they had stopped at a small country inn. A bright and forthright young boy offered them tea since his father, the proprietor, was out picking herbs in the mountain. The samurai explained how both his master and himself had been captivated by the boy's honesty: trying to steep the tea as his father had taught him, he did it with care and joy, patience and mindfulness—all without any affectation. The master later said the tea tasted so pure for that reason—the boy was unusual in that he wasn't at all embarrassed or trying to impress them. Though he made mistakes, they were natural and only brought grace to the liquor. He didn't need to apologize for the tea he spilled. His innocence was there in the tea, and the samurai thought it delicious and memorable.

The second samurai spoke of the time he had drunk tea with a famous tea master, whose skill in tea preparation rivaled any of the greats in history—even Master Lu Yu himself. He used the highest quality tea the samurai had ever seen. He heated the water in a pure silver kettle and steeped the tea in an ancient clay pot and equally old cups, painted porcelain with bright blue dragons. The liquor was exquisite, coating the mouth and throat and lasting on the breath for hours. The Qi also was delightful, and he could remember feeling it course through his limbs even late that night as he lay down to sleep. The lingering sweetness had impressed his soul, lasting til that very day they walked beside the stream.

The last samurai said that if they would deign to indulge him, he would save his tale for the following afternoon—if they would meet him at a certain time. Curious, his two companions wholeheartedly agreed. They couldn't wait to hear his story.

The following afternoon he led them down to the city park, near the banks of the river where they found the rickety, old bamboo stall of the "Old Tea Seller", Baisao. He had a small wooden table and simple pots and bowls. The old monk had long ago abandoned his monastic robes, donning the white and black Crane Robes of the ancient Taoist hermits, offering tea by the roadside for donations. Through connections with his hometown, the only open port in the kingdom, he was able to get small quantities of rare teas from the Mainland—some even aged and deep. The samurai thought their friend wished to buy them a cup of tea to drink as he regaled them with his story, but the true tale had already started with the simmering of the kettle on the coals.

The old man's clothes were stained and his teaware chipped, but there was obvious grace and mastery in his hands—there for any that had the eye to notice it, and the three samurai definitely did. They soon forgot all about why their friend had invited them, slipping into the dark tea the master prepared. Some of the few who knew about his small stall bragged that while the famous Chinese master Lu Tong needed "seven bowls" to reach the Land of the Immortals, Baisao could take you there in one.

The tea transcended quality. It was neither simple and unaffected, nor refined and delicate. The samurai lost themselves in its depths, though the cups seemed shallow. Afterwards, they understood why their friend had invited them. The old master smiled, his eyes twinkling like a child's. They each put a coin in his bamboo tube, which read: "The price of this tea is anything from a single *sen* to a thousand gold pieces. Otherwise, it is free. I only wish I could give it to you for less!"

While the next pot is steeping

The word "Zen" comes from the Chinese "Chan", which is itself a derivative of the Sanskrit "Dhyana", meaning "meditation". Zen is meditation. But not in the sense of "contemplation". Actually, *Dhyana* could be translated as "being-onto". It means being an open space for awareness. In being-onto a cup of tea, the distinction between the I-subject and the tea is erased. Zen is this open space—direct and unaffected observation. There is no word in all the ten-thousand languages that can really capture it as such, though any organization of words might instigate it if you're in the right space. "Spirituality" also falls short, though it is perhaps a step in the right direction to recognize that the world is "spirit", rather than these clunky "objects" we think are so solid. Modern scientists have also verified that matter truly is energy, after all. Some people think that spirituality of any kind is hocus-pocus and wave it off as fantasy: "I'm an ordinary guy. I get paid, watch TV and date my girlfriend. I have more important things to do with my time," etc., etc. But who is really fantasizing? The one who is deluded into believing they can actually own things, living through virtual entertainment and not in touch at all with such obvious and very real truths as how fleeting a life on this giant rock whirling millions of miles the hour through space really is or the one sitting with complete sobriety, upright and aware as she quietly observes all the subtle nuances in a bowl of tea? (And that wasn't meant to be a rhetorical question—I'm really asking!)

As the Mahayana teaching in *sutras* like the *Prajnaparamita Sutra*, which emphasized direct, experiential wisdom, came to China and blended with the meditations and philosophies of Taoist hermits, all kinds of new approaches and spiritual ways were developed, including the first ever self-sufficient monasteries. These Zen monks were among the first tea farmers, in fact. And since that time the paradox of such direct, intuitive wisdom in the present, ordinary moment in opposition to the need for meditation—often called "Zazen" after the Japanese pronunciation—this illogicality has been central to all Zen thought and discourse. After all, why meditate at all if we are already enlightened? Wouldn't such practices then just be polishing the ego, using spirituality itself to be a brighter, stronger identity? Other masters, like Dogen-zenji, taught that when meditation is done purely, and for its own sake, that itself is enlightenment—and in that state it isn't "you" who meditates, but the Buddha.

The famous passing on of the bowl and robe from the fifth to the sixth patriarch holds a clue as to how we can transcend this absurdity, not metaphysically but actually. The fifth patriarch was getting old and it was time to pass on the staff. He suggested a poetry contest—the award being the robe and bowl Bodhidharma had himself carried from India, handed down from the very Buddha himself. The senior disciple Shen Hsiu composed a poem, which captured his understanding of Zen. He was, however, a bit trepid and decided to first tack it to the abbot's door anonymously. It read:

> *The body is a Bodhi-tree,*
> *the mind a stand of mirror bright.*
> *Take care to wipe the mirror clean,*
> *so there is nowhere for the dust to light.*

The next day the old abbot had incense burned before the poem, calling it brilliant. That night, after the evening meditation, he read the poem before the congregation and said that anyone who put this into practice would surely become a buddha. But in the middle of that night, a little kitchen boy named Hui Neng tiptoed to the abbot's door and tacked another poem beneath it. It said:

> *There never was a Bodhi-tree,*
> *nor a stand of mirror bright.*
> *So please do tell me,*
> *where is the dust to light?*

Despite the fact that the entire community was against him, the old abbot led the young man to a nearby hill and bestowed the bowl and robe on him, as he had indeed proved himself worthy of the role.

Commonly, this is interpreted to mean that Hui Neng "won", and that his poem was "better" or somehow "higher". But if Shen Hsiu's poem did not capture Zen, then why did the master have incense burnt before it and call it brilliant, admonishing his students to heed its wisdom? Obviously, the master understood and recognized Hui Neng's insight, even before it was written, so why would he commend Shen Hsiu's if he felt it was incomplete? Also, according to the legend, the fifth patriarch instructed Hui Neng to travel south and spend the next years in retreat, practicing—so again why would he recognize Hui Neng's insight on the one hand and tell him to go practice on the other? Are the two poems really antithetical? Are they mutually exclusive? Can only one be true? And, finally, did Hui Neng's poem really trump Shen Hsiu's?

Perhaps Hui Neng's natural grace or deep understanding of Zen allowed him to penetrate the issue. But it was not, as is often proposed, that he outstripped Shen Hsiu. That is not why the abbot gave him the robe and bowl. No. The true power of Hui Neng's poem is in the relationship between the two poems and the way they compliment each other. One does not negate the other; instead, they dance together as partners. And this waltz is Zen—when the music is so great that both partners forget themselves and their roles, merging into the Tao itself.

There is a very real sense in which you cannot put energy into a future, enlightened "you". The ordinary life, living here and now is already *it*—this tea you drink is Zen practice, without remainder. And yet, philosophically this falls short, becoming at worst a justification to do anything you want including excess or laziness. While Zen would not judge debauchery, neither would it justify it—no matter what intellectual acrobatics you can perform, the monks of old were all chaste, practicing temperance and moral uprightness. Zen does offer spiritual freedom—to interpret the precepts as you would—but it does not shirk the consequences of behavior either. This doesn't mean there necessarily is a judgment or even the need to believe that the universe is karmically interested in our moral behavior, as some do; it is only to say that actions have consequences, and we are not able to foresee any of the unraveled ends of our actions, which spiral off and affect the world in myriad ways. The precepts are, in their purest form, but more skillful means—*upaya*. Actually, when you are pure, all that you touch is pure. There is no real formula for purity, just as there is no 1-2-3 recipe for Zen tea. I like St. Augustine's simple advice regarding our moral base (*sila*): "Love, and do what you will."

The innocent boy in this cup-story is beautiful. He is our buddha-nature, free of mind and its burden. He needs no discipline or practice. How can you practice being what you are? He is spontaneous and unaffected. He is the brush behind Hui Neng's poem. But his purity is short-lived: soon the vicissitudes of life will solidify his ego and he'll grow separate from the world before his return at death, or by grace in transcendence. He makes great tea because his mind doesn't tamper with the moment. It's almost as if the preparation were a natural extension of the tea bush's growth. There is indeed harmony in such a cup.

Then there is the expert of the second samurai's story. He has mastered the Cha part, but hasn't yet realized that tea prepared in this way always falls short, even if it be only slightly so. No matter how masterfully processed and prepared—no matter how great the tea and teaware—without the Tao, Cha is still in the material realm, and therefore often inspires greed and possessiveness. Most (not all) such Tea men (*Chajin*) end up lost in snobbery—without realizing that in Nature, beyond the mind, leaves are just leaves. The quality they value so highly is mind-made, in other words. In Zen, such "experts" get busy huffing and puffing their 'isms' and schisms, arguing the fine points of what is "True Zen" and who it's taught by—just as the former kind of experts do with varieties of tea and teaware.

Finally there is the true master, Baisao, who has learned the ways of the world and is wise. He meditates and understands Zen because he has read scriptures and books. He also has great skill in his hands, brewing the tea expertly and with grace. He knows the ins and outs of tea, and can caress the best out of it in all circumstances. Nevertheless, he is not lost in the "Cha" part of Cha Tao, which only leads to snobbery and materialism; but neither is he dreamy, lost in the "Tao". The Cha and Tao of Cha Tao must each be balanced. Too much Cha leads to possessiveness and greed—stuff we're using to fulfill some sense of lack. But tea is also not escapism, and neither is Zen, so too much focus on the Tao leads to cloudy, blissed-out meditations that are too far from the daily life. The master is grounded in Cha Tao, with skill in meditation and the material side as well. All the subtle additions he adds in technique and the great teaware he uses add up, and the cup is so refined you barely feel the tea liquor passing through your mouth—though it coats the throat and stays with the breath for hours to come. This tea is more refined, deeper and wiser. His mirror is clean of all dust: it shows you your ego and asks you to look upon it with insight; look upon it and realize there never was a mirror.

The real, indescribable Zen, is beyond the whole distinction of quality. In this space—the truly "enlightened" space, so to speak—there is neither enlightenment nor delusion. The innocence and mastery have merged and the paradox is resolved. That is the space between the poems, where they fall hopelessly in love with each other's eyes. There are then no more isms and schisms; no more agreeing or disagreeing. You can't disagree with Reality—not when it's fully present. There are many *koans* where a student says that he heard something like, "Bright and clear are the hundred grasses; bright and clear our ancestor's teaching" from some other master. The student then asks the master if this is correct, and the master answers that it's a terrible excuse for an understanding of Zen. When the student then asks the master for *his* understanding, he replies: "Bright and clear are the hundred grasses; bright and clear our ancestor's teaching!" Though the phrase changes, this formula repeats throughout many Zen parables. The master is attacking the student's tendency towards distinction itself—the division is itself the issue.

Sometimes we have to wait for the right catalyst to come about— the right smack on the face or cup of tea. Then everything falls into place. There is then Zen in the tea, sparkling just near the rim where the liquor turns golden, but no Zen in the mind. Master Rikyu's name, given to him when he was ordained, is a testament to this since "ri" means "sharpness" and "kyu" means "leisure", "rest" or "non-doing". Zen is a sharp leisure, an adroit rest. Zen is Rikyu.

It is the mind
That aspires
To set out onto the path
That is my very own
And revered master.
        —Attributed to Sen No Rikyu—

The Seventeenth Cup
The Cloud-covered Moon

Have a cup

Rikyu's son was cleaning the garden path—the *roji*—in preparation for an evening tea party his father was hosting. He carefully raked up all the fallen leaves and disposed of them. He weeded the flowerbeds and sprinkled fresh water on the plants, as his father had taught him to do. He then called Rikyu to examine his work.

"Not finished!" the old master exclaimed. His son therefore went back to work, knowing very well by then how much of a perfectionist the old Zen master was. He weeded between the stones on the path, and cleaned up some stray pine needles he had missed before. This took him another hour or so.

"Not finished!", the master again bellowed after he inspected the garden. Rikyu's son surveyed the garden more carefully this time. He picked out some of the wild flowers and raked the dirt in the beds so that it formed patterns of concentric circles. He scoured the garden and picked up even the smallest leaf or weed. He even sheared the grass so that it was all even. He smiled, proud of his work. The garden was cleaner than he could ever remember it being—surely this was enough. He once again summoned his father.

"It is getting late," sighed the old master, "and you haven't time to learn of yourself how to clean the garden properly. The guests will be here soon. Let me show you." Rikyu calmly strode over to the large tree that grew near the fence—its branches adumbrating the *roji*. He reached up and grabbed a large branch, and with a strength that belied his age shook it vigorously: a many-hued autumn shower raining down all over the path.

"That is how it's done!" He said, striding confidently inside.

While the next pot is steeping

In Zen art the aesthetic goal is called "wabi", a word that was originally used in poetry to refer to a feeling of the "cold and withered" or even "lonely and forsaken". Over time it took on a more positive tone, especially amongst tea cognoscenti: *Wabi* is the beauty in chaos, the perfection of imperfection. *Wabi* is at first an acceptance, and then later enjoyment of insufficiency. There can, after all, only be enough when there is enough. In a boundless, endless universe of eternal space, form can go on forever—insufficiency is a natural part of this existence, in other words. But the *feeling* of lack is mind-made, and no amount of stuff—no organization or situation—can ever fill it. Human dissatisfaction is of the mind, and freedom from it is also, therefore, in the mind. And in that freedom we find *wabi*: the ability to appreciate and revel in insufficiency. When we're hungry, we eat, knowing that in life the filling and returning hunger are central to this form and without them there could be no movement at all. Isn't that revolution from emptiness to form to emptiness beautiful?

The great tea master Takeno Joo was once asked what *wabi* meant and he said that we should look to a famous poem by a master named Teika:

> *As far as the eye could see*
> *Neither cherry blossoms nor maple leaves.*
> *A rush hut by the shores.*
> *Dusk in autumn.*

The cherry blossoms and maple leaves are symbolic of Nature's splendor, here suggested to the mind by the words but empty from Reality. The imagined brilliance makes the simple hut much more evocative. Another master named Soeki would put calligraphy of a second poem by Fujiwara Ietaka (1158-1237) in the alcove, next to the one above, believing that it perfectly embodied Master Rikyu's *wabi*, in part by responding and relating to the other:

To those who yearn for cherry blossoms
I'd like to show the first grass of spring,
Emerging from the mountain snow.

Ietaka's poem also captures *wabi* well, forcing us to see that the beauty of a few blades of the greenest, dawning grass poking through the white snow are in a way more beautiful than the flush summer green—for the contrast and sparkling relationship of emptiness and form that is the Zen ideal. Soeki is asking us to recognize the power in the distinction created by comparing this to the first poem: to look beyond even the imaginary concept of cherry blossoms and maple leaves, used in the older poem as a contrasting background, to the reality of form and formless before us in the *real* world.

The distinction between "pure" and "impure" is mind-made. The Buddha said once that the Road—both literal and metaphorical—doesn't mind whether the golden shoes of a prince or the dirty hooves of the ox tread across it. What could be more dirty than dirt? And yet, doesn't a cleaned and weeded flower bed sparkling with morning dew provoke a feeling of cleanliness and purity? Since ancient times the full moon has been used by Zen teachers and poets to represent enlightenment, since it reflects the sun's light without a trace of self. However, Takeno Joo so lucidly pointed out that the full moon slightly covered by silver-trimmed clouds is all the more beautiful. And that relationship between cloud and moon, enlightenment and delusion is all of what Zen is about, especially as communicated through *wabi* art.

We must be careful in our descriptions, though. There is no deliberate *wabi*. Being in the present moment, grasping Zen, the artist always expresses herself in spontaneity, as does Nature. This cannot be understood because an idea cannot be used in Zen art, or arguably at all: you cannot use the equator for anything, because it is just an intellectual abstraction. Neither can the number three do anything, having no reality outside the mind. Similarly, the idea or understanding of *wabi* cannot move the hand in a way that manifests genuine *wabi* in tea preparation, the composition of poetry, calligraphy or any art.

You can't *practice* any ideal, in fact, just as you can't *practice* Zen—you have to be it! That is why Zen is more of an art than a religion—a state of being rather than dogmas, ethics and/or theologies. And yet, this living wisdom is found in all traditions: Jesus didn't *practice* compassion, he *was* compassion! If you practice being humble, you set up a game where you actually think putting yourself beneath others is higher, and as such make a fool of yourself (and not the graceful fool the master portrays). Similarly, you cannot practice *wabi*. You can't *make* things look gracefully imperfect. It is their natural state, just as it is yours. *Wabi* is the revelation of that natural state, so that we see things as they are—*kensho*.

In this modern age, people often prefer the hedged, trimmed and squared garden—and its order—to the forest and its seeming chaos. The landscaped garden is appealing to the logical, rational mind. It seems as if Nature has been organized and controlled by man—instilling a false sense of security. In the forest the order is subtle and beyond comprehension—loosely organized by ecological currents we can never completely understand. Which is more beautiful? Which is truer?

Being human is to be rational. Denying the mind is not Zen, and not what *wabi* is about. *Wabi* is simplicity and natural grace, but not in opposition to the human element. On the contrary, Zen would include the human touch as a part of the Tao—an extension of Nature. The rational mind enjoys a bit of order. This itself is natural. We are a part of this world, not separate. The seasons still dictate our lives, as they once did, however boldly we try to ignore them. It is wonderful to enjoy the freedom of the woods, untouched by human development, but that enjoyment itself brings the human eye into the woods and participates in it. It is good to put the mind aside for a while and see the beauty in the untamed forest. The Zen master would love a quiet stroll through the park, but that doesn't mean she wouldn't also smile at the crafted garden.

The Zen garden, as a paragon of all Zen art including tea, isn't about removing the human touch and letting the space be overrun with weeds. That would have a kind of charm all its own if it weren't at all contrived—as it is with some old houses. Otherwise, why not strip naked and have tea in the jungle, drinking out of a coconut bowl? The Zen experience is communicated through art when the artist herself disappears—gets out of the way—and the Tao itself unfolds through this world. The movement, then, is spontaneous and unaffected. Rikyu calmly scatters the leaves, in recognition that he is as much a part of nature as the wind is. When the human effort is so in tune with the nature of the garden that they blend together naturally the garden is ready.

The best tea also demonstrates this aesthetic dialogue between human and Nature. The Chinese word for tea has human right in the middle. The best teas are grown and processed by people who know how to converse with Nature—their presence fully accepted as but another factor in the mountain ecology. They are tea, in other words. And then in the hands of the tea master, the preparation also culminates this extended hand—from out of the mountains, sun and moonshine, river water and mists, through the plant to the hand that makes it; and then on to those who drink it and make it a part of the human body. From Nature it sprouts, is tended by people and drunk in a return to that softness. Could you say the tea drinking is then less natural than the bushes' growth?

When you see that the *roji* is more beautiful with some leaves covering it, you will understand also how perfect the clouds over the full moon are. You don't intrude upon Nature, for that would be an intrusion upon yourself. How can you trespass in a universe without boundary? Though we cut this world up into plots of land we buy and sell, the lines are really imaginary. We don't own this earth any more than we own the bodies we live in. And neither are we aliens from some other dimension who come here for some time and then leave. This life is all that we are, and it flowers from out of this very earth—to which it will one day return.

Accepting the pure and impure, distinction vanishes. Befriend your impurities and they are no longer enemies. The sage has no enemies, no matter how others feel about him: "Forgive them, for they know not what they do." He is open and trusting of this world. That openhearted trust is Zen; it is *Dhyana*—being-onto the world. The true *Chajin* is a *man of tea*—he never refuses an invitation to tea and his house, his home and his heart are open to any guest. There is no locking the tea gate—it's rickety and couldn't keep anyone out anyway.

Zen is a seeing of things as they really are, and accepting the Truth no matter what it is. What is, *is*! Fighting with Reality only causes confusion, delusion and ultimately—when the Truth finds a way of rushing in, no matter how strong you think your mind-castle is—in the end suffering will result when our fantasies are contradicted by Reality, by the way things *really* are. Acceptance is powerful, and once you have seen things as they are (*Dhyana* = Zen = *kensho*), you can then trust completely.

If you fear people and the world, locking your doors, you need some clarity. This Zen-clarity is the skeleton key, opening all the doors and windows so you can see how boundless a world this is, and that all the locks were just the ego's way of creating a false sense of security. The only true safety is in Truth, just as real freedom means having no walls or chains to imprison you. The greatest palace belongs to the king who sleeps free of house and possession, for the sky is his roof and the earth his home. Find a home in the Tao, and you will truly be Immortal. As such, there is no longer any guest or host, for all are welcome inside and there's room for all and sundry.

What is it you fear from a guest, a stranger or enemy? Are you afraid that if you open your house or heart they will steal something from you? In seeing Truth, you should know—deep down in your marrow— that you never, ever owned anything to begin with, not even your body, which is composed of borrowed atoms. So what could your guest take from you? How can something that never belonged to you in the first place be taken away? This is why most spiritual traditions the world over abound with stories of sages chasing after a thief to give him the last treasure he forgot to take.

Or do you fear that if you open your house and heart you will be harmed bodily? Again, Zen-clarity wipes off this dust: you don't own this body—of the Earth and Sun it came into being and borrowed its energy and it will soon enough return hither, just as your being and mind arose into form out of emptiness and will ultimately dissolve back into that emptiness. And don't you want to welcome your death when he comes? Isn't the end "our only friend"? As we discussed earlier, those who have lived well receive their death into their house as but another welcome guest.

Dhyana is this open acceptance of any moment. In tea we say the guest and host vanish, in the realization that they are one and the same. And as tea and Zen are one flavor, it is easy to see how this metaphor of "guests" and "hosts" is not just in reference to people arriving to our tearoom for a tea ceremony, but to any "guest": any situation in our lives, met forthright and with all the graciousness of a host that has "forgotten guest and host". "Make yourself at home!", you say to the world as it comes in. In that way, even thinking is ok. Even thinking and dramatizing—that is what minds do.

Don't deny your creativity from this world out of some kind of close-minded fear to participate: scatter some leaves across your garden path and take your seat in the tea hut, being sure that you sit upright with all the composure that dignifies your place in this world. My master often asks if we are museum curators or kings. Museum curators collect stuff and information, and dust it off each day, happy to discuss their tidbits with other like-minded collectors. They don't realize they are participating in the world even behind all those locks and keypads, glass and sterility. Kings allow the world's wealth to flow through them, appreciating things and sharing them with others. The king sits down with poise, as naturally and regally as the wind that also scatters leaves each autumn.

Hundreds of feet of stones
Thick with moss!
Tea brewed with such water
Would attract few guests;
Yet seeing the moon reflected
In its midnight depths
Made me revise
My low opinion.
        —Wang Yu Cheng—

The Eighteenth Cup

I Raise my Cup and the Universe Turns

Have a cup

On Mount Wu Tai, the monks had just finished their long winter retreat. After months of silence, the master would then check on each disciple to see if they had any questions, also provoking them to demonstrate their progress. The first spring days had come, the mountains thawed and the air was warm and clear.

Starting with his most senior disciple, the old master invited him to go out to his favorite cliff for some late-morning tea. They sat beneath some pines and drank a few cups in silence, watching the clouds pass, some below their Heavenly seat.

"This teapot is the container, and there is the golden liquor inside it right now," began the master, "without moving the teapot, pour me a cup."

Without any hesitation, the student picked up the pot, leaned over and filled his master's cup. The master smiled and drank his cup. He presented the old pot to his student and bowed. He was a student no longer.

While the next pot is steeping

The master in this cup-story wants to see if his student understands "non-duality"—not one and not two. The answer must come from that space, though it doesn't matter what it is. He could have poured the tea over his own head, danced, shouted or even smacked his master—so long as it was with Zen awareness.

The master is in essence saying that the container, or circumstances of Reality around them, has within it the golden tea liquor—their individual, egoic minds. Can he pour the cup without moving the individuality, which is to ask does the movement of the world disturb the contents inside? Is the Truth affected by the changing forms?

People often identify completely with the contents of their lives, focusing exclusively on the experiences: sights, sounds, smells, tastes and thoughts. The ancient Indian scriptures called the *Upanishads* say that these percepts are "what people here adore". "But", they continue, "The wise see Brahman, Ultimate Reality, in the *awareness* that sees… hears… etc." We are not any one sight, sound or smell, in other words, but the *capacity* to see and hear itself—pure unaffected awareness prior to any percept. It is *upaya* to recognize the pure mind that allows us to experience as an aspect of our self, perhaps truer than any of the content. It is useful to rest in such emptiness; it brings peace and flourishes insight. Many of our problems can be avoided by not identifying so strongly with experiences that really are not a part of who we are. Otherwise, the realm of content has a way of corroding more and more of our life: As the ego expands its sphere to "my" and "mine", people try to also control others—things, people and situations—and then get frustrated by an obvious inability to do so; or not for long anyway.

It is obvious that we all have eyes and ears, though we are often deaf and blind—focused completely on the external, and ignoring the awareness that is at the heart of our experience, we are unable to really be open to what is happening around us. The great tea master Takeno Joo complimented Rikyu by saying: "You are not an ordinary man, but have ears that hear and eyes that see—the ability to perceive—and as a result your virtues are without taint." When you understand the pure space that allows us to really see and hear, that very ability to perceive, you can then appreciate how great of an honor Master Joo is bestowing on the younger wayfarer. The most famous of Chinese stories also sings of this. The master zither player, Po Ya, searched the world over for someone who could actually hear his music. Though many applauded, none really heard it. Then a simple man named Chung Tzu Chi heard him play and really felt the mountains in his mountain song and river in his riversong. When Chung Tzu Chi died, Po Ya severed his lute strings and never played again—such was the power of transmission from one heart to another when the ears were really open.

But Zen goes a step further than all this, suggesting we drop both—neither identifying with the content nor the container. In Zen, the individual and environment are not two. You can never understand any organism without understanding its environment. All phenomena are embedded within circumstances that weave out into an endless knot that connects the whole universe—the Tao. Subject and object, or metaphorically the river and the plants and animals that live in it, the Earth and all life on its surface, are all a "single"—for lack of a better word—interdependent Reality. That is another way of understanding the emptiness in form. You can't separate the fish from the water—lest it die and decompose into other elements—just as you can't separate the golden liquor from the pot, or from the universe for that matter. So how can the liquor be disturbed? That would mean the whole universe was disturbed.

If we were to list all of the conditions that make this teapot exactly as it is, here and now in the concrete, amongst that very, very long list would be the monks themselves, for were the teapot in someone else's hands it would not be this very teapot *as it is*. The essence of the teapot is thus emptied into its conditions—it doesn't have any independence to be "disturbed", in other words. Zen masters have said that dropping a pebble into a pond changes the entire universe, as the ripples carry out into eternity. Just as we are indistinguishable from our environment, those environments are also connected to others, and so on. Everything we do—even the smallest act—echoes in eternity.

The ancients understood clearly that our delusional addiction to mind-made dilemmas wasn't just based in the assumption that form (*rupa*) is real and the presumption that we see "objects", but also in language itself (*nama*). They therefore called the World of Dust: "nama-rupa". One of the greatest problems inherent in our languages is our use of nouns. We call it "tea" and then think that "it" moves when the pot is picked up. But if you look at a small sprouting tea plant, that is "tea". When it grows into a large bush it is also "tea". The leaves that are plucked are "tea", as is the final processed leaf we take home. The liquor in the cup is also "tea". Actually, in truth, "tea" is not a thing at all; *it is a process*! You could divide any of these stages into infinite parts intellectually, though in reality they are a single continuum from sprout to liquor. And this process of "tea" could not exist without the process we call "sun"—burning, glowing radiant explosions of countless hydrogen atoms; or the process "man"—the one who forms it all; the one who names it.

The monk knows that the container and content are not two, and there can therefore be no disturbance in the content by moving the container, just as the movement of planets, suns and people does not disturb the space of the universe which contains all this movement. There is no difference between the movement and the space within which it occurs. As individuals, we are also such movements—small ripples on the surface of a vast ocean. And though these waves have a certain uniqueness and individuality of their own, for some time, they are not separate from the ocean, but composed of it—flowing out from and back into it. Time, and the change it represents, is not distinct from space.

Raise your cup and the world turns because of it. Your tea is the movement of form within emptiness. And the emptiness and form are really not two, just as you are not really distinct from the tea, which will soon be inside you—a part of you. At first it seems like the tea is outside, separate; but then you drink it and absorb it. Where does the "tea" end and the process of "you" begin? Actually, this absorption is our true self, not some googly-eyed architect-ego behind the controls of our experience, but emptiness—an openness into which the world is poured. Where has it gone? What has it become? Did the world really move at all when the cup raised and the liquor flowed down your throat?

To live is to know the infinite universe,
though its creative forces remain forever unknowable.

—Zhu Xi—

The Nineteenth Cup
A Royal Steed Tethered Outside a Rush Hut

Have a cup

The great tea master Takeno Joo was retiring from the World of Dust. He'd learned tea in the affluent studies of merchants and civil servants, but the quietness inherent in the Leaf had whispered to him, goading him to the mountains and a simpler life. He had been a civil servant for fourteen years, though he'd had his eye on the mountains for much of that time. He built a small hermitage to practice his tea and meditation and withdrew in farewell.

After the construction was complete, Master Joo criticized some of the design in the tearoom. The size was not to his liking. He wanted the hut to be smaller than a traditional tearoom. Also, the alcove was not the right size and he hoped to border it with driftwood from the nearby coast, rather than the costly wood his students had used. He went and gathered this wood himself, hoping that his students would return with the craftsmen and help fix up the tearoom to his requirements.

The only thing he had brought from his old house in the city was a bamboo peg with a unique shape, used as a hook to hang scrolls in the alcove. During the creation of the initial tearoom he had hung it up himself while work was still going on. While the master went for a final visit to some students in the city, his students and the carpenters put the tearoom back together in the way he wished. However, they accidentally covered the hole the master had made for the bamboo peg, forgetting to mark it. The carpenter came and measured the height of most scrolls, and from memory they replaced the peg where it had been—give or take a centimeter or two.

When the master returned he was joyous and bid his students welcome anytime to his hermitage for tea. He thought the work they had done was amazing and complimented them profusely, saying the tearoom was orders of magnitude more beautiful and special having been built as a gift. Finally, when they were leaving he patted his senior student's back and smiled, "except the peg is in the wrong place... It's two centimeters too low."

While the next pot is steeping

There is in Zen a natural disposition towards simplicity that grows over time, like the slow wisdom of a beard. As we identify more and more with emptiness, we find beauty not just in those things which are obviously beautiful, but in the subtler realm as well: drops of dew, broken pots, cast-off furniture, driftwood and stones, etc. A large part of why these things are so beautiful is that their beauty doesn't inspire a desire to posses, which some other kinds of beauty so often engender. There is no inclination to follow the deluded invitation to possession when looking across the surface of a stone or the grain of wood. The value then is in the stillness within them, and us, as well as the patterns they reflect—often eons of oh so patient natural forces. A cracked old pot doesn't call out to be owned, and yet what an amazing flower vase it would make. Things return to life in this way, which is but Nature's way of gathering here what was spilled over there.

The modern World is cluttered, if it's anything at all: cluttered cities full of cluttered houses and people with cluttered minds, rambling on their cluttered cell phones about which clutter to put where, when and with whom. But how are the things that feel so "cluttered" any different from the things in "Nature"? What is the difference between the junk in the ubiquitous "junk drawer" and a pile of stones? What is it that tatami inspires in us that linoleum just can't?

We are like birds in a cage made of our own minds. We think we're trapped in bodies that die, and very serious drama that everyone must understand, and quickly! Some fishermen named Wang who lived in southern China five hundred years ago had some serious drama, too. Do you want me to stop and tell you about it? No. You don't care. "But… but wait," you protest, "this so-so did this and it is very serious business!" People literally huff and puff when they tell you about how important their drama is. Is it really? In a universe that doesn't even bat an eye at stars thousands of times bigger than the Earth erupting in explosions big enough to engulf our whole solar system? When you step back from the drama, you may notice that the door to the cage is open. It always has been. We're not locked in. And then, stepping out, we see that actually there wasn't ever any cage at all. Our hands pass through the bars.

Zen is much more about stripping away than it is about adding anything. Lao Tzu also said that the Tao the sage follows is a taking away, the World an adding on. We don't have to read *sutras* or agonizing *koans* to get Zen. Neither do we have to buy robes or beliefs, and especially not meditation cushions or gilded buddhas. "Your mind is Buddha," said Bodhidharma, "so you don't need a buddha to worship Buddha." A cup of tea will do just fine.

Zen is also much more about the letting-go than it is about learning or any of the other spiritual catch phrases, like "insight" or "enlightenment". We cast off the body and mind. The real withdrawal from the World of Dust is this detachment. And it isn't just about letting go of the clutter in our homes, but more importantly (or perhaps exclusively) the clutter in our minds: opinions and beliefs, thoughts about the way we think people or things "really are", thoughts about "clutter" and "simplicity"—even the idea of Zen as an 'ism'. The ego loves its beliefs and opinions, and considers an argument against a dearly held belief as threatening to itself. Actually, truth be told, there is no understanding Reality. It's too big for that. Anything we understand is relative and partial. And so we let go and things just have a way of getting simpler and simpler.

It's sometimes hard to really appreciate the art in a museum because there are too many masterpieces on the same wall. A true work of art fills a room, and needs to be viewed alone. Recognizing and learning to utilize space in art is the Zen ideal, as it is in the art of living as well: the white paper of the scroll painting or calligraphy, the empty parts of the stage in theater, and in teaware also there is empty space within the bowl or cup—around the handle, button and inside the teapot. So also in music and language there are spaces, and without these gaps the notes/words do not make any sense. The space speaks as much as the ink, in other words. Still, it is important to remember that Zen is not the simplicity of the desert or windswept field per se. There is grass poking through the snow. Removing the human element completely is okay for a mountain vista or sunset at the beach, but it looks contrived in painting, ceramics or architecture. It is much better if the human pattern is as natural as the growing grain of the wood it sculpts, moving flawlessly with the message that was already in the wood, waiting for the extraneous parts to be removed. We are like that, too: blocks of marble with buddhas inside. The buddha is already there, we just need to take off the unwanted chips.

There is a spontaneous, go-with-the-flow naturalness in life that we all follow, but in Zen the softness is buffered by a sharpness that is highly aware. Nothing gets by the Zen mind, though it comments on little and sometimes may seem to not be paying attention. Though our minds grew out of this world, it is through all the cracks and paradoxes that we come to realize the distinction between the two isn't real. It all seems nonsensical and witty, relaxed and haughty, but it's serious and adroit as well. Master Joo said in his "Twelve Precepts of Tea" that if your style is too elegant, you appear wanting, and if too *wabi* you appear slovenly. The freedom and simplicity of Zen is not an attitude of anything goes, though it is okay, in fact, for anything to happen.

The "shinkantaza" of Japanese Zen is often translated as "just sitting". But it doesn't mean just sitting around. There's a difference between meditation and couch surfing—between the spurious leisure to pursue some mundane pleasure and the very real freedom when absolutely nothing is lacking from the moment. It is the posture, you could say—the upright mind and body. "Shinkantaza" is often used to scold students who are too focused on the goal—keep it simple, in other words: just sit. It is easy to look at the cluttered life and think that the simple, clean life of a master like Joo is miles away. It makes you want to give up, or worse dream of future enlightenments experienced with fireworks of supernatural powers. Neither can someone else do the job for us. The clutter is our mind-made self, and only we can clean it up. There are spiritual Michelangelos, who carve resplendent buddhas from their marble blocks, but we all have to do with what we've been given. No master can carve your buddha for you.

Sometimes, to avoid these stumbles you have to simplify your simplification process itself. You clean a house one room at a time, or even more concretely one spot at a time. Lao Tzu said that the wise man always and ever deals with challenges when they are small, before they've had the chance to develop into something difficult—small weeds are deftly plucked. And as things get cleaner and cleaner, simpler and simpler it is true that all the stress of the clutter evaporates, but small details also become more and more important as well. You are relaxed and calm, naturally so, in a clean house—though to stay so, you must also be alert and diligent in your cleaning at the same time—*shinkantaza*. Master Joo's life is incredibly simple, which is why the details matter, and why he notices them at all.

Like all the great tea masters of Japan, Takeno Joo spent a lot of time learning Zen, and was himself a novice monk. It is difficult to express the Zen life—mindless, directionless, purposeless and without beginning and end. Sometimes, it's better to look at some Zen art: poetry, painting or tea. It may just grab you in a way the words can't. Master Joo's tea hut does this as well—it's more Zen than a lot of temples.

It may seem on the surface that the hyper-sensitivity of the master is snobbish and betrays the simplicity he's building. On the contrary, it is because he is so simple that no detail escapes him. This is in accord with Nature, which is also sometimes hard and sometimes soft. The soft-spoken, gentle spiritual master who smiles and looks stoned is either drifting in some meditative state that cannot be sustained, or more likely acting—playing a role they believe will help them, or perhaps help others.

In simplicity we appreciate the stillness inherent in objects. This is the "beginner's mind" so revered by Zen masters, which though open and unconvinced of anything—waiting for the Tao to begin the dance—also seems to have a natural grace, even as we bumble through things like a beginner. Objects then become like friends: when they visit and are close we adore and are grateful for them, in reverence of their beauty; and then when it's time to go we say farewell gracefully, knowing they have a journey of their own, which ends elsewhere.

There's no way to enhance who you are or your quality of life by being around any person/thing, and when you stop using people/things as ego-enhancers they are much more beautiful, and rewarding to be around. There is then a compassion for this world, and sensitivity to its beauty. The cultivation of this capacity of quiet detachment and aesthetic sensibility is the very reason why a life of tea is also a life of Zen.

Tea is very simple: leaves and water. It flows from the pot naturally. You just tilt the pot up and the liquor flows out. That's its nature. But the awareness is complete. There isn't any tension between the two, though they can be viewed intellectually as in opposition—calm opposition. This is the mindfulness of Zen. It doesn't mean strained concentration or one-pointed mind, but rather poise in action, natural simplicity with detailed decoration. The Tao in the tea was there long before tea was ever picked and steeped by man, just as buddha-nature was spread across this earth long before Sidhatta Gotama was born.

Taoist hermits loved cranes, and the tradition of watching and painting them spread to Zen as well. Taoist monastic robes were called "Crane Robes" and were black and white for this reason. The crane has a large body relative to its wire-thin legs, but it can stand on just one of those legs for hours in perfect balance. It needs no flattery to be regal; no affectation to be graceful; and definitely needn't add anything to its nature to enhance its being. It seems asleep, unmoving in unflinching relaxation. But when a fish passes, it flashes down and scoops it up. And then you realize that it was really very aware the whole time—it's just that its awareness was so in tune with the world, you mistook it for unconcern. Actually, the detached mind is not only the one capable of the greatest concern, but also the most effective when it comes time to act. It is this uprightness that the monastic contributes to the world, though it seems like his hermitage offers nothing to society.

Master Joo is here communicating a simplicity and communion with Nature—a hut made of rush, tatami and driftwood. But he is also aware of every single detail. Calm and yet poised, we make our tea like the crane. Balanced on one thin little leg, we uphold our lives, detached from the World but not drifting in other, imaginary worlds either. Fully "in the World but not of it." The crane's leg is fully in the muck, holding its mind just above in perfect poise. Occasionally, it dips down to snatch up a fish.

When you simplify your tea, the small details become even more important. You notice things your guests would never see. In that way, the tea isn't bounded in the tearoom anymore. Every detail of every aspect of your life is tea preparation. The practice of tea is then free of itself as a practice, just as it is more Zen than Zen since it has cast off all the Zen robes and mannerisms, buddhas and mass-marketed cushions—which "stink of Zen" as they say—and replaced them with so many cracked old pots and cups. The Way of Tea is solitary, in retreat, especially from tea and the Way of Tea.

Men of tea especially hate to be seen as such.

—Takeno Joo—

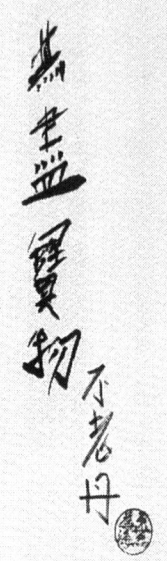

The Twentieth Cup
A Kingly Gift

Have a cup

The palace spires turned through ornate colors and patterns until they suddenly splayed out towards the sky like the swift turn of a brush stroke. The great red roof peaked above the whole complex, crowning the Lord of Heaven and Earth that resided within. Every detail of every building, garden and fountain had been perfected through the centuries. It was a great worship of Dynasty. If it was possible for man to be divine on Earth, it was possible for him to hope his way through the drudgery of a poor, rural life merely miles away from this luxury. In fact, the farmer didn't even mind sharing half of his all-too-meager income in order to pay for one of the small stones used to ornament but one of the many fountains that he and his kin would never see. Why? Because the proximity of possibility brightened his world, gave luster to his clouds and dreams to his sky. Having a man of flesh and blood between the Earth and Heaven balanced things and assured the people that the Sky would hear their prayers. Sometimes, when the sun was setting, the farmers would lean on their hoes, wipe the toil from their brows and smile at the shining buttresses, towers and sweeping wings of the palace roofs. There were grins of contention. Heaven wasn't that far away after all.

It is amazing that millions of such farmers would all be forgotten, endlessly so. The craftsmen and artists, whose great passion and patience had crafted all the glorious inspiration in the palace would also be lost. All the servants and cooks who orbited the Emperor like lesser moons, the counselors and administrators that discussed matters of state, the eunuchs, wives and mistresses to fulfill his paradise—all would be eclipsed and erased in times to come. For the only one that mattered in this world was the one that walked barefoot across the strewn flowers that the nameless servants had spent all morning gathering; the one—and only one—permitted to wear the yellow silk that had been so cautiously woven and stitched to perfectly fit his golden and divine form. Thousands of hours and tetra-watts of power had all been channeled into this effort to make bliss of his reality. Was it possible for such a man to see beyond the walls he wasn't permitted to cross? Could one bathed in milk and stuffed with delight ever realize that he and the dirty farmers he'd never seen both came into the world in the same kind of bloody spasm, and that they'd surely leave it the same too?

For most of the Emperors that came before and after His Highness the fourteenth Song Jing Xiang, the detachment brought on by a life in the palace only brought forth the desire for political power, expansion, conquest and glory at best, and decadent waste at worst. The monks taught that attachment to material things led to suffering. None of the emperors had ever had any issue with that lesson. It is difficult to have desire for material wealth when you're surrounded by paradisiacal beauty that appeals to all the senses. And what does it matter when anything given, taken or broken is always replaced in kind, often with a newer and more beautiful replacement. Most emperors embraced their terrific power and reveled in their ability to move great forces with but a word. They relished in victory over foes they had never met, increase in wealth and land that they would never spend or visit. It was the power itself surging through their very veins that enthralled them, not the property. Other kings, like Song Jing Xiang's father, ignored the world and grew fat and drunk as they more and more spread their arms and crashed backwards, adrift in the great sea of hedonism that surrounded them everywhere. They seemed happy and carefree, but where hardly alive. History often dispatched of such kings, as they didn't fit the illusion needed to justify the great expense necessary to make the Divine City. His father had been fortunate, though, and had lived all his days in peace, dying suddenly in middle-age from what everyone knew was just his vices catching up with him.

It had seemed almost surreal when Song Jing Xiang, but a young man, had sat and watched the great ceremony that ordained him as Heaven's representative on Earth. He had tried to be just and wise and rule his people with their interests at heart—to be everything his father had not been. But much of his power was just ceremonial. There were administers, councilors and governors that controlled much of the world with little more than reverence and symbolic gesture to him. He probably could have swept up all the power had he had the initiative. His heart just wasn't in the venture. He couldn't work himself into the frenzy needed to care enough to seize power and crush any obstacles and opponents. His disposition was far too dreamy-distant.

From an early age he had loved one teacher above all his others. He was a senior accountant in the treasury and a Eunuch. He had long ago been the boy-prince's arithmetic teacher. In between abacus lessons, they would sit and drink tea. The emperor had always had an interest in learning how to do the small things that emperors were supposed to have a servant do for them. He immediately took an interest in the process of making tea. His teacher learned to award concentration during his math with lessons in tea preparation. He taught the boy which hardwood made the perfect charcoal. He showed him how to make the flame consistent with just the right amount of ash. Later, they would try different kettles of pottery, metal and then silver and gold, tasting just water to learn the differences each made. Though the boy wasn't permitted to leave the Forbidden City, the old teacher described the mountains and springs the water and tea came from in such detail that the boy could close his eyes, flare his nostrils and envision life there by the river, mountains and sky. He longed even then to lead an ordinary life, with an ordinary wife, children; perhaps a farm and some animals that would graze freely nearby. Of course, his visions of pedestrian life were as celestial as the palace, but he was a boy and had never known hardship. He was caught serving himself tea at the age of ten, but the emperor only dismissed the issue. He told the court-appointed nanny, a burly eunuch named Tung whose only pleasure in life was the pride and honor he felt on the rare occasion when he was given permission to turn the royal buttocks red, to let the boy be. For the most part, the emperor ignored his son, spoiling him the way he did himself. "Let the boy make tea like a servant. It's quaint." He even made a joke of it at parties. If he had only known that the dismissive waive of his hand would upset the whole empire in prophetic ripples, starting with his son playing with the royal teaware and leading to a time of turmoil followed by a complete change in Dynastic power... Of course, Life dances upon a desert of 'if-only' grains...

The boy's teacher, Yang, had smuggled in a purple-sand clay teapot from the nearby village and given it to the prince on his twelfth birthday. It was so very ordinary, nothing like the ornate porcelain served to him. He reveled in its simplicity. To him, it was the most beautiful thing in the whole palace. It connected him to his dreams. He would stare for hours at the scrolls in his mother's antechamber, the old yellowish ones with paintings of distant mountains and waterfalls. He had always been told that the palace was Heaven, but to him the mountains that danced down those scrolls were miles above the highest roof of the hall where court was held. At night when the last servant left his quarters, leaving behind a single lamp so the boy wouldn't be afraid of the dark, he would creep over and reach under the cabinet on the wall to retrieve the hidden bundle of silk there. Forgetting the need to be quiet he would bound back to the bed and sit cross-legged, carefully unwrapping his treasure. He would rub the little teapot and admire the gorgeous curves of its spout and simple handle. He could notice the slight burnish that increased with each and every use. He would rub it with the silk wrapping and smell the inside, longing for the rare breaks in his math classes when he was free to use it. His teacher would tell him of the craggy Wuyi Mountains near his distant home. He said they really did spin and turn, dancing towards the sky like they did in the paintings. The boy would sigh and dream of his little wooden house without any Tung, or court ladies, long dinners, lessons or endless occasion. He longed to gather tea leaves, collect water from a stream up a path that would start near his cottage. His life there would be so gloriously ordinary that in those brief visions he would come to believe that he was in fact closer to the gods than anyone else. To look at the boy as he closed his eyes and daydreamed of the mountains brought the old teacher great joy. He taught the boy how to taste the different teas, showing him the differences between the green leaves, the balled Oolongs south of his home, and the elegant striped teas of Wuyi. These were the boy's favorite. He wondered why the court always drank brick tea with milk or butter when there was such glorious tea as this in the world. Then again, his father had always favored rice wine, even during the day when others were drinking tea. He vowed to change that when he was emperor. From then on the tribute teas would be worthy of the throne.

When the boy reached his teens he still wanted to drink tea with the very old teacher, even though they had finished school. He would often ask about Yang's life before the palace. He wanted to know every detail about how the food was cooked in the village, what they did when the roof leaked, and what their beds looked and felt like—everything. The old eunuch loved the boy. His kindness had brought favor to the accountant within the palace staff and made his life easier. Everyone knew the boy would be king one day, and that his favorite teacher would surely have great power then. He also loved to reminisce about his family who he would never see again. He was more than happy to spend the afternoon drinking cup after cup and recounting all the details of life below the great spires of Wuyi. After all, it would serve the emperor well to know just how his people were living beyond these walls.

As the boy grew older his duties increased and he began to visit the old teacher less and less. He was there, though, when the old servant died. He held his hand and cried, thanking him for the tea. The old man smiled in understanding. He had been more of a father than his own had ever been. He was entombed with all the honor of a regent…

The grown emperor stared down at the simple teapot that now fit snug in the palm of his hand. It was smooth and shiny in the moonlight, shades of purple smeared with silver glares that made it seem almost magical. It had always been so to him. Though his world since birth had sparkled with the brilliance of every shade of gem, it had all seemed to be nothing more than glass, as though the whole rainbow palace was painted on the surface of an eggshell that a single flick could shatter. Only the teapot had ever had real beauty. It was solid, earthy—and yet hollowed sky within. It had been used by some villager for years before being passed on to him. Hundreds of times had leaves been gently placed within and steeped with water, the pot steaming in peace as the aromas released their serenity and brought comfort to the villager, or so he imagined. Then he had treasured it and it had served him too, though not with a sense of luxury, comfort or ease the way it had its previous owner. The pot had been his wings; for it was on the gilded spirals of steam that he had flown over the palace walls to the secret cottage in his mind. He gently held the robes in the drawer aside and placed the teapot below. Only the king was allowed to touch this dresser, these robes. He stood still and voiced a silent prayer that the teapot would continue on through time, bringing joy and peace to its next owner and all those beyond. He reached in his pocket and squeezed the metal there until it hurt his palm. He remembered his teacher. He remembered the hours in the sun drinking green tea, the games of chess and dark aged tea with the rain pounding on the roof and drooping the flowers. He could see his master's wrinkled hands twisting the lids off the endless little ornate tins he carried in his robes, and smell the tea. His master had laughed at his excited huffs of the tea. "Breathe deeply and slowly, inhaling its elegance gently", his teacher would repeat each time. And each time, he would revel in the reward of listening.

One afternoon, after a few hours of quietly drinking tea, the master would tell him how he had used his influence to get a copy of the key used to open the kitchen gates the foods were brought in through to be inspected on their way to the royal table. He said he had used half of his salary throughout the years to have the best teas brought to the palace to share with the boy. When the boy offered to compensate him, he only shook his head and said that one day he would pay him back and then some. The boy had promised to grant the old man any wish when he became emperor.

The emperor squeezed the metal in his pocket as the yellow robe slipped from his naked form and slithered to the floor in a soft pile. For the first time in his life, he allowed a coarse brown cloth to touch his flesh, passing over his raised fist that still held the metal shaft, its string thong dangling down his arm. He remembered squeezing the old teacher's hand as he died. The old man had smiled and beckoned him near. In a raspy voice he had said, "When you're ready, go to my room and find the jar with my best tea. You'll know the one. Brew it once for me. That's my wish." Though he had died some time later, those had been his last words. The prince had declared that his rooms were to be left untouched for all time.

Swept up in duty, years had whirled by. He'd been married to a princess from the North, though she hadn't yet borne him a child. He was thankful for that now. He had buried his father and sat as the pomp and glory of his kingdom paraded before him. Even then he felt hollow. He had tried ruling for some time, using his visions of Wuyi and the people there to guide his decisions, but he was too easily steered astray into daydreaming by the advisers that coveted power over the state. His greatest teacher had taught him too much about Heaven and too little about the ways of the Earth.

Years went by and he had all but forgotten his master's wish. Then, one afternoon as he sat brewing his tea with his treasured pot—it was now a royal edict that the emperor would make his own tea with purple-sand pots, thousands of which had poured into the city in tribute when it was found that he loved them, but none of the ornate masterpieces even approached the beauty of the simple one his master had given him. He sat brewing a good Wuyi tea that had just been given to the court and wondering where in Heaven his teacher was. That's when he remembered the wish. He cleaned the pot and ran off to his teacher's corridors. Servants had to drop things to make their observances as the emperor surprised them, dashing by. He found the rooms just as they had always been, though covered in dust. He grabbed a rag and cleaned off the shelf of jars that the teacher had kept all his teas in. There was row upon row of elegant silver and gold canisters, beautiful porcelain painted with hours of reds and blues and other fineries, many of which had been gifts from the emperor himself. He knew which one held the best tea right way. It was a simple brown clay pot with a stone lid. No carving decorated its walls, no glaze or paint highlighted its curves. The emperor smiled and cleaned off the old tea table. He washed the old kettle as the charcoal heated up. When everything was ready he poured the last of the great, aged tea out on the table. A glimmer of gold and a metal ding surprised him. He set the pot down and brushed the old brown leaves and their dust aside. There beneath was an old, worn brass key…

The emperor quietly pushed the last gate aside. He stepped out into the open air and smiled even at the compost heap that jutted up against the nearby palace wall. He looked out towards the horizon, closed his eyes, sighed and flared his nostrils just as he had done as a boy. A lifetime of teaching. A lifetime of tea had paid off. The old master had his wish…

While the next pot is steeping

In the tea space, prince and pauper are equal—both men who must live and die in this world, following its rhythms. Social status, race, job, nationality and all other such roles can indeed have a real effect on our lives, but they are—in essence—mind-made. They are not who we are. Even the emperor, who thinks he is a god, still eats and defecates like a man, same as any other. The Buddha was a man, not a golden statue or something supernatural. And if the tea is steeped the right way, the Buddha, a prince and a beggar drink together without distinction.

All of our functions begin with a small f. Even an emperor—or today's equivalent, a millionaire or movie star—is just a small f. No matter how big you draw a small f—across a football field—it will always be a small f. The president is a very big small f, function, whereas a waiter is a smaller one. But they are both just functions—roles people play, things they do—not who they are. What, then, is our Foundation, big F? What is our "Face before we were born"? Do we even have a purpose? An essence? And if so, could it be expressed?

Emperor Hui Tsung really did prepare tea with his own august hands. Some emperors also traveled in disguise throughout the city drinking tea, beginning a tradition in China that continues today of tapping the table when tea is served—a secret bow, "Kou Tou", to the disguised emperor. Though it was forbidden, these emperors sought the ordinary beyond the palace. And what an image to pour in the cup, holding and gazing into its depths: of the emperor in some hidden corner of the palace preparing tea with his own simple pots and cups—the very same kinds of tea we can enjoy today!

Through tea we can start to look beyond our story—our role and history; our drama and all our phony-baloney histrionics—to the real pith of our lives: the stuff we are living, breathing, eating and drinking. As such, the warmth of the cup isn't another experience we've collected to tell others about. It isn't another page in a diary; it's just this physical warmth, as it is. The sweetness on our breath and the Qi flowing through us aren't points of departure into metaphysical obnubilation; but just this very stuff—this suchness. It doesn't matter if you are in kindergarten or at the top of a hundred-story building in the penthouse, not to the tea anyway. Our musings together throughout this book can lead you to that brink, to look out at the vast and open sky. Can you leap into the unknowable? Otherwise, all these thousands of words are but baubles—playthings of divided-mind, seeking whole-mind.

In tea we are all monks and nuns, leaving behind the World of Red Dust. There's no delusion here. We are ordained through this ceremony, casting off our faces and games—lastly and perhaps most importantly dropping the whole "Zen" game itself. When the tea is pure, there is no need to discuss its "Zen flavor". If the two are one, then they aren't distinct anymore—life is Zen and Zen is life and we don't even need call either one by different names. "When body and mind are dropped away, with no ground to stand upon, acts of lofty grace and solitary influence."

In the Japanese tea ceremony, practitioners often speak of the "essence" as the teaware that doesn't move—like the kettle, flowers and scroll—and the "function" as that which does, like the bowl and tea scoop. But this is only to see the outer, material sheen without penetrating to the Zen flavor of tea: the real "essence" is our true self, unmoving and complete Tao; and the "function" is all the changing forms, including the tea session itself.

With a bit of perspective we can see further and more vividly what our Foundation—big F, rather than small f, function—for walking on this Earth is all about. There is a joy in this Way of Being—a tremendous, tear-filled sense of wonder. Could anything be missing from such a moment?

When all is complete and nothing wanting, there are no more functions of "self" as ego. Tea is just tea, and words slip away. The cup finds itself alone, with no one to enter and become. But it doesn't mind—literally it *does not mind.*

When the soul is pure and the cha clean,
There is no one left for the tea to drink—
Alone in the garden,
Steaming to itself.
                              —Wu De—

The Last Cup

The Ten Lost Tea-brewing Pictures

I

The Wayfarer Begins His Search for the Great Tea Bush

Aimlessly wandering, seeking the Leaf—
The Mountains widen, the gorges deepen.
On and on, with wearied heart he roams.
Not knowing where to look,
He rests, for a moment, by a stream
And listens to the evening cicadas.

Following the Way of Tea, the first real step must be taken alone, and with a true devotion to the Truth. We get entangled, confused and the world of tea seems so complicated, looming above us in every direction. We've heard told of a tea tree whose leaves can be brewed into an ethereal draught, and a single sip is enough to kindle the Tao in any man. But we know not where to turn. Actually, the Tao was always with us, and there was never any need to travel anywhere—every aspect of our daily lives is already the Tao of Tea. It takes a heightened perspective and the experience of a master to see this, though. In that way, a separation between the seeker and sought arises, and in delusion the desire to be "awakened". Earnestly, he sets out on his journey. But all is not lost—the time away from home will do him some good.

II

The Wayfarer Finds Scattered Signs

Near a chanting brook,
Some scattered bushes cling to the cliffsides.
They hint at what aromatic teas must grow
Deeper still,
If he could cloudwalk to higher peaks.

ourneying deeper into the Way of Tea, we find some books, magazines and lectures to learn from. But having no experience of our own, the tracks to the Truth are scattered. Some say this teapot is authentic, others say it is a fake; some name a tea "high-quality" and others tell us it isn't worth drinking. If we were in the Tao, we wouldn't be dominated by anyone's words, knowing the Truth ourselves. Without experience of our own we vacillate. We must travel higher to gain vision and perspective. We haven't yet really entered the Tao, just appreciated the art others have used to express their experiences along the trail. It's good to study what the masters now and long ago have left behind for us. These scattered signposts assure us that the path does, in fact, lead somewhere, inspiring us to travel on. It is important, however, not to stop here—busy collecting signposts rather than journeying on to the Great Tea Bush and drinking that cup we set out to find.

III

A Glimpse of the Great Tea Bush—the First Sip

Its branches crowned
With emerald leaves and trilling yellow warblers:
A warm calm in such verdure—
All the ten-thousand words
Could never describe this place.

Further down the path, the wayfarer finds the bush from which the Elixir of Immortality is brewed and tries that first, unforgettable sip. This is the point at which the spiritual pilgrim stops aping the masters of old, and understanding becomes seeing—but just a glimpse. Having tried a great tea that is alive, the drinker is pacified and the mind silenced. This peace is transcendent, powerful. At first it seems as if this quality is in the tea, teaware or perhaps the knowledge and expertise of the master who prepared it. But at this stage of the journey, we turn down the most important bend—towards the within. We realize that the calmness we experience is within, just as the Way of Tea, in all its meanderings, traverses the wide-open forest of our heart. An encyclopedia of books could never teach this, because the intellectual signs we had studied previously—the books on tea and/or *sutras* on "Zen" as a kind of Buddhism—only hinted at its whereabouts. To see it, we had to set aside these pointers and walk on, around this bend. We can't stop here, though, for we've just caught a fleeting glance of the Tao. There is great joy in this experience—warm, green peace—and it is nice to take a rest in the true knowledge that the tea we've sought really exists and we know where to find it, but we must move on to the source.

IV

Grabbing the Kettle, Making the Tea

Plucked leaves,
Water and coals,
Can't prepare the tea.
One cup amongst the peaks—
Clear and golden-tinged—
And the next clouds to mist again.

As we practice living tea, our lower-self doesn't vanish altogether, but rears up in craving for expensive tea and teaware, and jealousy of those who have more or have realized more. Even after some years, and genuine attainment, it's so easy to become a snob, scorning beginners and the tea they enjoy. What you condemn in others' tea really just says more about your own tea. There can be no complacency. Now that we've gotten hold of the Tao in that Great Bush, we mustn't let go. Sometimes we realize that all the tea and teaware we've accumulated are all wrong. A great self-doubt arises and we want to smash the pot and walk away. The teachings are losing their meaning. All our books on tea, the notebooks and journals we've written detailing our experiences, are all so much scrap paper—good for kindling or to "paper bare walls". All our practice seems to crumble to dust. This is a time for transformation: to stoke a powerful resolve in our own hearts and forge our destiny. The trivialities of tea fall away at this stage and we lose interest in collecting tidbits of information or useless teaware. The mind and the Path towards its pacification become all-encompassing. Sure, we have found the sacred bush all sages have sought, but making the Elixir wasn't as easy as we thought. Because it is in our minds and hearts, it isn't enough to just grab the leaves and gather some water; and yet that is precisely what we must do. This "dark night of the soul" is all the darker before the dawn. Through tea, we break our habits, sacrificing them to the Goddess of all Herbs.

V

Alchemy

Sun and moon,
Rise and fall
Round his cups of tea.
Pot by pot,
Inner and outer alchemy
Begin to concord
In distilled harmony.

The Enlightenment that comes after drinking the Morning Dew is fleeting. Now that the passions are tamed and the realization fulfilled, there is still a lifetime of quiet uprightness to be lived. We come to realize that the Elixir of Life was always within us, not in the tea. The outer alchemy—the harmonious blending of the water, fire, tea and teaware—has been achieved, unlocking deeper cups than ever before and settling the mind into its natural stillness. Though the mind is pacified, there are still years of habitual delusion to contend with. At this stage we have settled into a life of tea, and are completely comfortable with our own abilities. But we mustn't allow our attainment to make us complacent. Old habits can revive at any time. We must continue practicing, humbling ourselves before each and every tea session. The old Taoist masters said: "The embryo of the sage is long in nurturing." It will take time to hatch. For now, we must calmly warm our inner egg, shower our pot with steaming water and preheat our cups. Daily, we align our tea and selves with the Tao and let each session come and go in peaceful, yet vigilant routine: Days pass into months, and months into seasons. The real secret of the masters is that they never miss a day of practice, no matter how natural their talent may seem.

VI

Returning a Teaman

Farewell to mountain tea,
Crags and cliffs,
Clouds at dusk.
Back to the hut,
Where the ordinary rice kettle
Sings from above the fire-pit.

What was realized has now become life as lived. The tea was never important, the bush never any more sacred than the bowl, the rock or the man; and yet now we are truly tea-masters—men of tea (*Chajin*). The Immortality the Elixir promised was always there, around and through our lives—communion with the undying Tao. With practice, the hands have reached a true concordance with the Tao and it prepares our tea nowadays. There is no more need for mountain heights. We can return home, knowing that the struggle was just an imaginary game we played when we were young—true and false, right and wrong all mind-made delusions. All of our worry and pretension when making tea were stumbling us up. We were getting in our own way. As soon as we set down the whole journey and became "Teamen"—Tea and Human, one and the same—a single process of brewing and looking, drinking and living arose. We were so poised before that there was still a trace of the old tension. We still relied on that certain tea or teaware. Now we know that "as long as there's a kettle, we can make tea." Even our simple village kettle will do. The Tao is as much in the mountains as it is in the hut. Now we can appreciate how beautiful the ordinary kettle's melody is, without seeking out remote songbirds.

VII

Transcending Tea, Only the Man

At home in his hut,
The morning sun has risen
But still no one has stirred.
His pot and kettle sit idly by,
Quiet as the figure in the shadows.

the last picture, the man and tea have become one—the subject and object merged. But here we advance beyond this oneness. Realizing that the Tao is within, the *Chajin* no longer needs a guide, knowing there is nowhere to be guided to. Not only have we set down the teachings of the masters, which only point at the moon, but here—in this seventh stage—we are free from all lingering habits, at rest. In Zen, as in Tea, we first practice the rules, following the masters; then break through the rules to the inner meaning—the Tao to which they refer—and finally, at this stage, reach a freedom from the rules. Paradoxically, this freedom is not bound by the rules of practice, though it still follows them. In other words, we aren't chained to the rules anymore, but keep them of our own volition, naturally and without effort or discipline. Having mastered all the elements that go into tea preparation, there is now freedom to change them, adapting to whatever situation arises. Even when we're not drinking tea, the Tao of Tea is still unfolding and we are still capable of expressing its truths. We are no longer relying on the tea as our sole form of communication with the Tao, or to express it to others. Anything will do. Like the Buddha's raft, we no longer need the tea, having reached the other shore—having realized the buddha-nature was always here—the Way of Tea began long before the first leaf fell into Shen Nong's kettle.

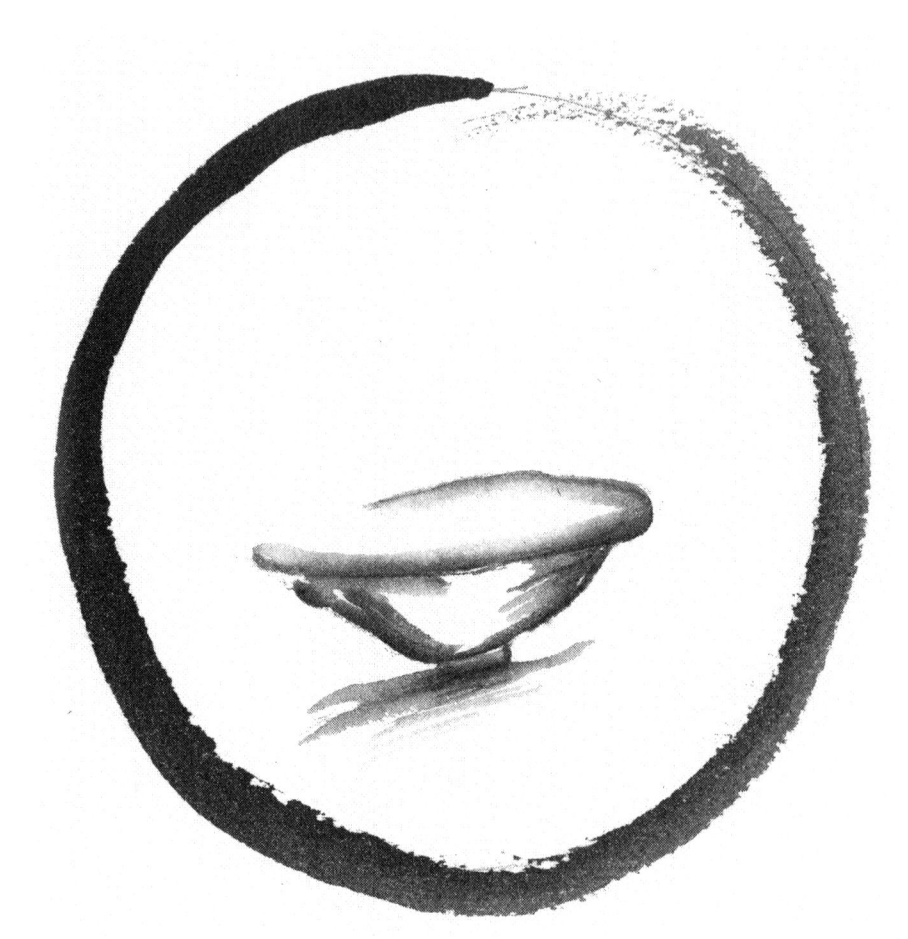

VIII

Transcending the Man, Rinsing the Tea

Emptied tea bowl,
Full of Heaven—
How could anyone
Cross from rim to rim?

We have sought after the Great Bush we heard could brew the Elixir of life, and we found it. We processed its leaves, mastered its ways and then freed ourselves of them. We've even forgotten them completely. But until now, we hadn't forgotten ourselves—the one constant element throughout the whole journey. Now we've returned to the emptiness out of which our whole lives came forth, let alone such a spiritual pilgrimage. But how is this emptiness different from the one before we came to be? How is this innocence different from that of the butterfly or songbird? What has changed in this endless Tao now that we have come and gone? Been born, searched, found, trained, freed and forgotten? Has the journey left a trace?

IX

A Return to the Source

All his tracks vanish
When the snow melts.
Better to have never gone?
Who can say if there's
No magic in the mountains,
Simply mountains around the hut;
No stillness in the tea,
Simply leaves and water?

In the beginning, the emptiness and void cracked, flooding with light and form. Who can say why? As a human, he can't rest in emptiness for too long if he's to be alive. But you cannot say the form "returns"—for now he has neither attachment to emptiness nor to form, and without any hold on form, he cannot be "reformed". There was never any *one* to be reformed: "First there was a mountain, then there was no mountain, then there is." Nature's floodgates open and the Tao moves through the all—the spring has bubbled up, the river flown down the mountain, found the sea and evaporated into empty, endless Heaven. But now, at this stage, the rain has fallen once again—a warm spring shower that nourishes everything: The kind you can dance in. Now, the tea really *is* tea, the mountain really *is* a mountain and the man truly *is* a man. There never was a journey, not really. When you're thirsty, drink some tea.

X

Entering the Village, Empty-handed

A few scattered leaves,
A cracked pot and a cup—
With dusty, travel-worn robes
He sits by the village park
Brewing tea for passerby
Who've come to see the spring blossoms
Mirrored in the river.

Unenlightened, there's no point in staying here in this hut. Maybe another will find shelter in it, as he once did. Up to now the Way has focused on the liberation of the self from its own delusional existence. But that can't be all, can it? After all, the trip from the springwell of immortality, down the mountain to the sea—evaporating into space and raining back down upon the earth—has taught him that all are related, all connected: form in emptiness, emptiness in form. There is work to do. It's the Buddha's final challenge, as Mara whispers for him to "stay, rest for a while… find peace 'neath this tree." But he doesn't. He leaves the forest for the village—a farewell to the mountains, the Great Tea Bush and Morning Dew; a farewell to peace and enlightenment. He forsakes Immortality for a broken-down stall in the village where he serves free tea to passersby. Some of them put a coin in his bamboo tube. He doesn't mind. But he likes the ones who halt mid-sip, set the bowl down and look to the distant mountains beyond the village, as if they've just heard a sound coming from there. To these he tells the oldest tale: of a Great Tea Bush hidden somewhere beyond a bend, the leaves of which can be distilled into the Golden Elixir of Life. At such times he sighs, "Wouldn't that be nice?"

Acknowledgements

Without a first step there is no journey. Deep is the gratitude we must feel for the ones that catalyze the first question—the first stirring in the dream. My introduction to the East came through some of the most warm-hearted smiles the world's ever seen: I bow deeply before William Peters and Steven Laycock. May the spirit of generosity they embody travel on, to inspire all the ten-thousand others as they did myself.

Also, I'd like to thank Matthew London, Kaiya and Lindsey for their awesome help editing this manuscript. Deep hand-on-heart gratitude...

This book is for all those who have taught me about Zen and tea, and all those I have yet to learn from. May I never be too vain to learn from any person or situation, whether stray dog or village farmer. And may I never be too proud to offer guidance to any that seek it. May I never refuse an invitation to tea—no matter how far or difficult, may I travel hither as though my life and spirit depended upon it, as they surely do! May we all find the Zen in our tea, and the tea in our Zen!

Zen and Tea are indeed one flavor!

Have a cup

Made in the USA
Middletown, DE
23 June 2023

33373123R00109